WORKERS SAY NO TO THE SHAH

(Labour Law and strikes in Iran)

by T. Jalil

with

Foreword by: Bob Wright
(Assistant General Secretary, AUEW)

Published by CRTURI London, April 1977
BCM 816, London WC1V 6XX
England.

Iranian Workers Say No To The Shah:

Labour Law and strikes in Iran: by T. Jalil

Published by the Campaign for the Restoration of
Trade Union Rights in Iran. London. First print April 1977.

ISBN 0 905901 01 0

CONTENTS

continued.../

Contents, continued... Page

FOREWORD

IRANIAN WORKERS SAY NO TO THE SHAH: LABOUR LAW AND STRIKES IN IRAN

Foreword by Brother Bob Wright, Assistant General Secretary, Amalgamated Union of Engineering Workers of Great Britain and Ireland

Many Trade Unionists and Socialists in the United Kingdom do not always appreciate the widespread repression of basic human rights throughout the world, which take many forms and our preoccupation with our own grievances and aspirations often cause us to look askance at others, and sometimes overlook our influence and ability to render assistance and encouragement to workers in other countries.

IRAN is such a country, governed as it is by a despotic regime under the Shah and controlled by his secret police organisation, SAVAK, which is his instrument of repression and is totally under his control, with a very rich and powerful ruling class and conversely a very poor population, but through this blackness shines a struggling and brave new force of courageous workers and leaders who maintain the fight for basic democratic rights and in Britain the "Campaign for the Restoration of Trade Union Rights in Iran", CRTURI, are seeking support from British Trade Unions to ensure that we are aware of the facts and the role of western capitalism and multi-national companies who assist the maintenance of the "Shah of Iran" and exploit the conditions he provides to maximise profit.

This book is a welcome disclosure of the mockery of so-called Labour Laws, and protection in this corrupt society, it also discloses the role of the CIA and the state run official Unions and repression of genuine trade union rights, we should remember that in 1953, 'democracy' was crushed in IRAN and many thousands of students, socialists and Trade Unionists have either been murdered or linger in gaol in this relatively rich Middle East country, grinding poverty is rife, but still the struggle is carried on.

I have no hesitation in commending this book as a useful follow-on to the previous publication, "Workers of Iran" which provides an explanation and calls for your help.

With fraternal good wishes,

Bob Wright

AUEW.

April 26th, 1977

2. PREFACE

The activities of the Campaign for the Restoration of Trade Union Rights in Iran (CRTURI), and in particular the publication in July 1976 of our booklet WORKERS OF IRAN: Repression and the Fight for Democratic Trade Unions, plus the December 1976 circular which was sent to the Labour Party Constituency and Young Socialist branches, have led to various responses by the British labour movement.[1] Some sections of the movement have given support to the struggle of the working class in Iran for independent, democratic trade unions and one form of this support was to protest on behalf of their brothers and sisters to the Iranian Embassy (see Appendix I for an example of these protests and the complete text of the "Labour Law of Iran").
The reasons for these protests are that workers have:

no freedom to organise their own independent, (both from the employers and the state), democratic trade unions;

no freedom to protest about their often intolerable living and working conditions;

no freedom to form, or belong to, a political party of their own choice which could conform with their ideals and could help to change these conditions or take industrial action -

because when they do they are gunned down by soldiers or imprisoned and tortured by SAVAK - the secret police; in spite of all this repression the workers have intensified their struggle.

On the other hand, the Iranian authorities (at the Embassy in London) have responded by sending out to the protesters copies of the English translation

---

1. We find the pattern of response to our efforts interesting, and also the silence on the part of some organisations. We will return to an analysis of this at a future date.

of the "Labour Law of Iran", (plus "Iran's Programme for the Expansion of Industrial Ownership"[2]); and they have also offered Embassy-financed and sponsored and supervised trips to Iran for trade unionists to "study" conditions there under the noses of the secret police agents, but trade unionists have turned down such offers on valid grounds.

These activities of the Embassy have led us to write a critical analysis of the first of these two "weapons" of the Iranian authorities against those who are fighting for the workers' cause. The present work is an immediate response to "Labour Law of Iran". It deals only with the text of the law as sent out by the Embassy, not with any additions or changes made lately, and not with the new and very severe decree on work discipline issued by the Ministry of Labour and Social Affairs under Dr M. Azmoon whose anti-working class record is spotless. We feel that the publication of this work, which itself is a critical survey of Iran's Labour Law on paper and in practice is urgently needed by those who fight against the repression under which the workers of Iran live and work.

If the Embassy is going to continue to respond to British protests in this way, then the British labour movement must have the ammunition with which to fight back.

But we go further. The Shah has talked about the "illiterate" and "pathetic" workers of "his" country: we want to show how these "illiterate" and "pathetic" people are standing up to one of the most brutal regimes in the world, how they cope with SAVAK, the Shah's secret police which is responsible only to him and he in turn is responsible to international capital, and can use any methods of torture and intimidation to try and crush all opposition; how the CIA collaborates with SAVAK and tries to infiltrate the labour movement; and how they go on strike for better wages and conditions even when faced with bullets and bayonets.

---

2. A future analysis will contain a critical study of Iran's Programme for the expansion of Industrial Ownership. But we would make one comment: Hitler, like the Shah, talked about profit-sharing. cntd. following page...

Finally, we detail a few of the many protests and statements which are being made by British organisations - Amnesty International, the Labour Party, the TUC, and the grass roots of the labour movement; and deal with the question of trade union visits to Iran.

Appendix I contains the text of Iran's Labour Law; Appendix II gives a picture of who is on the other side, the blacklist of multinationals who have set themselves up in Iran; Appendix III reproduces a contemporary document on the early history of trade unions in Iran; and then we list our sponsors.

T. Jalil

April 22, 1977

---

2. cntd...

""Socialism" remained a slogan under the Nazis although in their programme they demanded the abolition of unearned income, the complete seizure of all war profits and profit sharing in large concerns."

(Our emphasis) The German Labour Movement DGB, Dieter Schuster, p. 69. Published by the German Federation of Trade Unions DGB, March 1973.

1. INTRODUCTION

> "Most workers want nothing more of the law than that it should leave them alone."[3]

> "This biased law administered in a biased way was another factor which explains historically the traditional hostility of workers to law, lawyers and the courts."[4]

The law in this country and in Iran will never be "equal" for both workers and employers; and existing unequal laws are not administered, interpreted and enforced strictly both for the workers and the employers. Why? Because the individual worker and employer wield unequal power.

> "Except in the most mechanical sense, there is nothing like parity or a possible equilibrium between an individual employer and an individual worker. The concentrated power of accumulated capital can only be matched by the concentrated power of the workers acting in solidarity."[5]

The prerequisite of equal law, equal administration and interpretation and enforcement is a form of socio-economic relations - a mode of production - which is lacking at this time in these two countries; in other words, socialism.

This inequality applies to every kind of law, whether it is labour, civil, or criminal.

Having mentioned this basic similarity between the two countries over labour law, we must now point out the gross dissimilarities between them.

---

3. The Worker and The Law, K.W. Wedderburn, Pelican, 1971, p.13.
4. Worker's Rights, Paul O'Higgins, Arrow Books, 1976, p.44.
5. Laws Against Strikes, Otto Kahn-Freund and Bob Hepple, Fabian Research Series 305, 1972, p.6.

The main difference is that in Britain the labour movement has fought for its own labour laws whether it was in the form of forcing the government to pass legislation which employers must respect, such as the 8-hour working day; or whether it was forcing the government to repeal laws which violated their basic rights, such as the Combination Laws or the more recent Tory Industrial Relations Act, 1971. In both situations the workers fought so that either the government or the employers, or both, would leave them alone since they could not protect them.

Those labour laws enacted and carried out in practice in this country today are due to the persistent struggle of the British labour movement.

In Iran at the present time the labour law is also the by-product of the past labour movement, such as the struggles and the victories of the printworkers and the carpet weavers; but the organised movement was smashed brutally by the father of the present Shah. Once again, after his deposition in 1941, until the CIA coup of 1953, the Iranian labour movement enjoyed a certain kind of freedom as compared with the dark ages of Reza Shah. Since 1953 the present Shah has systematically smashed into pieces the organised labour movement. The present Labour Law in Iran is the direct "gift" of His Imperial Majesty, the King of Kings, to his "illiterate" and "ignorant" subjects - the Shah claims to be the main prop behind putting this law into practice. It is true that the Shah's decreed law on the one hand reflects the interests of the big multi-nationals and the necessity for unbridled fast capitalist development in Iran; but on the other hand it is also a concession against the potential danger which threatens the tottering peacock throne from the workers. There is a third point; in 1961 the regime saw a possibility of a liberal bourgeois attempt to take over the government (demonstrations occurred and liberal slogans were put forward). The Shah cracked down on this sharply, seeing it as a danger to his position; but he is not above stealing some of his liberal opponents' ideas, such as those on labour law. And there is a fourth element; a unique propaganda purpose. This element expresses the Shah's consciousness of the judgement of the future; and he uses apologist historians and journalists to picture him as a benevolent, just king.

In the same way he produces "laws" which on paper look liberal and "progressive" (until one enquires into the conditions and the practices behind the paper face).

He also pretends to be interested in the opinions of others, even western opponents, on these laws. For instance, when a Trades Council delegation went to the Iranian Embassy in London in February of this year, to protest about the conditions of the workers in Iran and the lack of free trade unions, they were asked by an Embassy Economic Counsellor if any of their members had legal knowledge, and if so, would they please study and comment on the Iranian Labour Law "and make progressive suggestions". This shows how far the Shah, and his servants abroad, will go to put on a liberal face.

Because there is no organised labour movement in Iran yet even this inegalitarian law will remain on paper only. In order to put an egalitarian law into practice one must create those socio-economic conditions and relations which can guarantee the putting into practice of all its provisions. We would never be surprised if the Shah's government decreed the most liberal labour law of any existing capitalist state, at any time in the future: anything is possible when laws are the "gift" of the Shah. They are not worth one penny. The Iranian workers are striving to overthrow the politico-economic power of the present regime and establish their own independent democratic organisations.

We have not here dealt with the law in the numbered sequence of the articles; we have divided our consideration into various sections according to themes and sometimes even within these, crossing some dividing lines. Since the entire law is reproduced in Appendix I we will refer in the text to individual articles without necessarily quoting them in full.

2. TRADE UNIONS

Articles 26 and 29 of the Iranian Labour Law state that:

> "All syndicates, unions and confederations are bound, at the time of formation, to draw up a constitution and submit it to the Ministry of Labour for registration. The Ministry of Labour shall agree to the registration of such associations provided their constitutions are not in conflict with the provisions of this Act and its relevant Regulation."
>
> "Syndicates, unions and confederations shall not be entitled to interfere in political affairs. They may however in cases of safeguarding their trade and economic interests express tendencies towards and co-operate with political parties."

(Our emphasis)

These two articles violate flagrantly the most basic democratic rights of workers. According to the Philadelphia Declaration of 1944, which the ILO recognises as one of the

> "fundamental principles on which this organisation (the ILO) is based" :
>
> "freedom of expression and association are essential to sustained progress".[6]

And according to the International Labour Conference, 30th Session, Geneva 1947:

> "...freedom of association was to be guaranteed not only to employers and workers in private industry, but also to the public employees, and without distinction or discrimination of any kind as to occupation, sex, colour, race, creed,

---

6. Quoted in the Labour and Trade Union Situation in Spain, ILO, Geneva, 1969, p.230.

nationality or political opinion."[7]

(Our emphasis)

A second fundamental guarantee agreed to by the ILO was added in 1948 at their conference, 31st Session, at San Fransisco:

> "Workers' and employers' organisations shall have the right to draw up their constitutions and rules, to elect their representatives in full freedom, to organise their administration and activities and to formulate their programme."
>
> "The public authorities shall refrain from any interference which would restrict this right or impede the lawful exercise thereof."[8]

(Our emphasis)

These guarantees occur in the Freedom of Association and Protection of the Right to Organise Convention, 1948, (No. 87).

It is crystal clear that articles 26 and 29 of Iran's "Labour Law" contradict these principles set out in the ILO Convention.

Since article 29 was written, there have been some developments in Iran. All political parties, including those which were created by the government, have been suppressed, and the Shah has declared that only one party, called the National Resurgence Party, is to be allowed to exist and the Iranian Workers' Organisation - on paper the equivalent of the TUC - was ordered by the Shah to affiliate to his political party.

"The subordination of the trade union organisation to the state" is completed in Iran, to use an ILO phrase.

The ILO, which was investigating the labour and trade union situation in Franco's fascist Spain, on the question of freedom of association had this to say to the Spanish government:

---

8. Record of Proceedings (Geneva, ILO, 1950), Appendix X, p.477, quoted on p.232 of the Labour and Trade Union Situation in Spain.
9. The Labour and Trade Union Situation in Spain, p.243.

"...to draw the attention of the Spanish Government to the fundamental contradiction between the legislation in force in Spain and the principles relating to freedom of association..."

(which had been adopted by ILO)

"...to urge the Government to amend its legislation in order to render it compatible with these principles, and, in particular, with the principles that (i) workers should have the right to establish and join organisations of their own choosing without previous authorisation, (ii) such organisations should have the right to draw up their constitutions and rules, to elect their representatives in full freedom, to organise their administration and activities and to formulate their programmes, and the public authorities should refrain from any interference which would restrict this right or impede the lawful exercise thereof, and (iii) such organisations should not be liable to be dissolved or suspended by administrative authority; to draw the attention of the Government to the principle expressed by the International Labour Conference at its 35th Session (1952) in the resolution concerning the independence of the trade union movement that governments "should not attempt to transform the trade union movement into an instrument for the pursuance of political aims, nor should they attempt to interfere with the normal functions of a trade union movement because of its freely established relationship with a political party."" 10

(Our emphasis)

---

10. Ibid. p p. 243-4.

Article 27 gives a very narrow definition of trade union rights; only two items (a) and (c) try to say anything 'positive' about the workers' right to struggle for better conditions. One of the main criticisms of the article is that it is absolutely silent about the right to strike.[11] Very subtly, this right is denied through the imposition of compulsory arbitration - and where such arbitration breaks down the state steps in quite nakedly and says: (Article 46)

> "Where the two parties refuse to accept the recommendations of the Disputes Settlement Board within a period of three days, the Head of the Department of Labour is bound to report the matter immediately to the Ministry of Labour for adoption of the necessary decision. Where necessary the Council of Ministers may so long as the dispute has not been settled, operate the working place on behalf of the employer in any manner as it may deem appropriate."

(Our emphasis)

One of the fundamental weapons of the workers against employers has always been the right to strike. Without this right all collective bargaining is meaningless. If the workers have no right to go on strike how can they force the employer to come to terms with them? Consequently in this article there is no mention of strike funds. Those workers who dare to go on strike in spite of having the government against them, have to live on their own money - more correctly, have to starve!

Section (a) of the article gives the right to conclude collective labour contracts. It is clear that a "collective labour contract" which ignores the freedom to organise and to strike will be meaningless.

---

11. "... strikes (which are illegal) have begun to occur when in the past three months the Government has ineffectively sought to implement a wages policy." (Financial Times, Monday, June 21, 1976) quoted on p.34 of WORKERS OF IRAN.

Article 28 forbids coercion to accept or to prevent membership of a syndicate.

The Shah has said:

> "Those who believe in the Iranian Constitution, the Monarchial regime, and the principles of the White Revolution, must join the new party. Those who do not believe in these principles are traitors who must either go to prison or leave the country."[12]

So in one area at least, the political, the Shah does admit to a belief in coercion, and in one sense force is used against trade unionists: they have no option but to join the government-controlled unions if they are interested in belonging to a public - as opposed to underground - trade union at all.[13]

(a) LABOUR CONTRACT

Note 2 of article 33 states that a workers' representative should not be dismissed without the approval of the Ministry of Labour and Social Affairs. This article is designed to, and does, function against the workers' fight for their own genuine representatives. How? As we have already mentioned, the state attempts to control the trade unions. The state tries very hard to ensure this but of course they cannot always succeed; workers use their own ingenuity and creativeness to deceive the enemy, i.e. the secret police, which watches the so-called elections to make sure that "undesirable" or "subversive" (that is, those who would fight for their fellow-workers) workers are not nominated. When such workers are nominated, pressure is put on them to withdraw, and if they refuse they sometimes conveniently disappear before the election.[14] When this happens the secret police put

---

12. WORKERS OF IRAN, p.46., using a quotation which appeared in the Guardian, Saturday, February 19, 1976.
13. Because there is a tendency amongst trade unionists to carry out their activities underground.
14. Because of these and other abuses of democratic process, one tendency which has appeared amongst the workers is for all their activities to go underground.

up their own stooge for election as the workers' representative and make sure that he succeeds. They also use agents to influence the voters, to express support for particular candidates.

British workers used to their own trade union elections know that only members who fulfil the constitutional provisions of their union can take part in meetings and elections and outsiders are not permitted to interfere directly. Under these conditions of duress and fear the SAVAK candidates are often elected. But not always. Sometimes they fail, despite trying hard, and this is an important source of inspiration and hope for the workers for their struggle because they know that if they study the conditions and understand the mechanics of their own repression, its causes and effects, and if they organise themselves and become united they can defeat the most sophisticated secret police. Although the workers may not want these unrepresentative people who are foisted on them they find it hard to get rid of them because the government protects them by this clause which insists on the agreement of the Ministry before any "representative" is changed.[15]

Article 32 states that any party cancelling a contract which had been concluded for a definite period shall be bound to indemnify the other party. Every worker in this country knows that they sign a contract agreeing to certain wages and with certain conceptions about future rates of inflation in their minds. Let us assume that the rate of increase of prices starts to zoom and becomes higher than the expected rate. Despite this, the worker must continue to respect his contract with the employer, otherwise he will be liable to prosecution and will have to pay for his employer's "damages" and "losses". Every British Chrysler worker knows how Chrysler did not respect the 'labour contract' moving their work to other parts of the world where there was more profit to be gained and declaring themselves bankrupt here, but nobody prosecuted a bankrupt company

---

15. WORKERS OF IRAN, p.56., tells how in the Meli Shoe Factory the workers went on strike and one of their demands was for a change in the so-called "workers' representative" who had really been chosen by SAVAK.

for not providing jobs or respecting the labour contracts.

Article 33 provides on paper for some protection against arbitary dismissal, allowing a worker with three months' service to appeal against dismissal and gain some financial compensation. The employer is given the option to pay this or to reinstate the worker.[16]

(b) COLLECTIVE BARGAINING CONTRACTS

Article 35 discusses collective bargaining. Collective bargaining is based on the assumption that there exist trade unions independent from both the bosses and the state and which represent the interests of their members fearlessly and without pressure. Since such trade unions do not exist in Iran collective bargaining is meaningless; and notice that the word 'free' is not used in this text.

(c) SETTLEMENT OF DISPUTES

Articles 37 to 47 dealing with the settlement of disputes, are extremely fascinating. If a dispute is not settled by the workers and the employer, then it has to be referred to the local Department of Labour office and within three days of receiving the complaint the Department refers the matter to the respective Factory Council. What is the composition of the Factory Council? Is it truly representative of the workers' interests? No. It consists of the genuine representatives of the employer plus the genuine representative of the Ministry of Labour plus the ungenuine or forced-upon-them-from-the-top workers' representative. The highly qualified Factory Council, or to put it more accurately, this employers' council, has to make decisions and pass judgements on workers' grievances. It is clear that even if the workers fought hard and gained their own genuine representatives they would always be outvoted by the combined votes of the government and the employer; in other words, workers are always in a minority on these councils.

---

16. Even this has proved too much for the government and a recent decree has changed these terms in favour of the employers.

The note to article 38 makes this even more explicit by stating that where a council does not exist at a factory the Department of Labour will make a binding award.

The Disputes Settlement Board has the same membership as the "employers' council", i.e. one employer, one government official and one so-called workers' representative. This Board is presided over by the Governor of the Area.

Note 1 of article 40 makes the position very clear:

> "In the event of a tie, the vote of the group which includes the representative of the Ministry of Labour shall be final and binding."

Article 44 specifies the procedure for the election of the representatives of the three bodies. The government and the employers can be left to themselves: the workers on the other hand, in practice find themselves "guided" by SAVAK agents, not always successfully, as to which people they should elect. Because of this attitude the workers' elections are nearly always manipulated but here and there a real representative is elected.

What will happen if the workers dare to question this judgement and decide that they can understand their own interests and refuse to accept the final verdict of the Ministry of Labour?

Article 46 has the answer. The Council of Ministers will operate the factory and force the worker under threat of bayonets to resume working. If they still resist and show determination a few will be shot dead to show the others what will happen to them if they question the greater wisdom of His Imperial Majesty.

Article 41 states that the worker has to pay for any damage which he causes to his employer through his own fault or negligence. Ignoring for the moment all the root causes of negligence such as economic and social and psychological problems which may affect workers, we concentrate solely on asking who will decide whether the responsibility for the damage lies in the worker's fault or in the employer's unsafe equipment? The answer is the well-known Factory Council or the Disputes Settlement Board.

(d) HIGH LABOUR COUNCIL

This article states that the members of the High Labour Council will be appointed for a period of two years by the Ministry of Labour.

The Council shall consist of three principal members (and their alternates) from each of:

1. The government;
2. The employers' syndicates with a minimum of 500 members; and,
3. Registered workers' syndicates.

In the case of the latter two the Minister of Labour appoints from nominees made by the syndicates.

The function of this High Labour Council is to give:

> "approval of executive regulations for the enforcement of this Act as well as carrying out any other relevant laws and regulations."

Does this article need any comment? We think not. The chain of control has by now been made so clear.

3. CONDITIONS OF WORK OF WOMEN

See articles 17, 18, 19 and 20.

Here again, British workers may be misled, since they are not familiar with how a dictator like the Shah can not only order the execution of trade unionists who oppose him, but also publish the most liberal labour laws. Once more it is instructive to compare the Shah to Franco, whose labour laws were, if anything, even more liberal than those of his Iranian successor.

Enactments

> "...forbid discrimination against women in apprenticeship, recruitment, tests, bonuses, promotion, and so on, and lay down that there shall be equal pay for equal work ... a woman who marries may choose between continuing her job, denouncing her contract of employment (in which case she is paid any relevant allowances), and leaving her job for a period of between one and five years, by opting for voluntary redundancy. In choosing voluntary redundancy, she is entitled to reinstatement in the undertaking, in the same grade, or in a grade below or above that in which she was formerly employed, as the management may decide."

Other decrees make it illegal

> "to employ women of any age, in certain industries and occupations considered especially arduous, dangerous or unhealthy."

If under 21 there are further restrictions. Women must be paid time and a half for overtime and,

> "must not work for a total of more than ten hours a day."

> "Maternity leave is described in the Contracts of Employment Act, under which female workers are entitled to six weeks' leave before childbirth; after childbirth, they are obliged to take six weeks off. Throughout the whole period, the employer is obliged to keep the woman's job open for her , and the period may be extended should the woman, as a result of her confinement, fall ill. While suckling their infants, women workers are entitled to one hour's break a day, which may be taken in two half-hour periods."[17]

---

17. pp.60-1 of The Labour and Trade Union Situation in Spain,ILO 1969.

As can be seen Franco's labour law is in some respects more liberal than the Shah's on the following points:

Franco:	Shah:
1. 6 weeks off after childbirth	4 weeks
2. women must not work a total of more than 10 hours a day	they can work up to 12 hours
3. overtime is paid at the rate of basic plus 50 per cent	overtime pay is basic plus 35 per cent
4. there is a specific list of industries where women must not work	there is a vague concept of "injurious" work where women must not work
5. work at night is illegal except in certain industries	work at night is illegal except in certain industries but it is added "and other jobs as will be specified at the discretion of the Ministry of Labour".[18]
6. a woman who marries may choose between continuing her job, leaving work completely or leaving for 1-5 years after which she can have the job back	no mention of this point

Nor does the Shah's "protection" for women workers take the real situation into account, e.g. article 17 on night work between the hours of 10 pm and 6 am even overlooks so obvious a fact as the climate - during the day in some parts of Iran in summer the temperature rises to 52-54°C (125.6-129.2°F). Therefore

---

18. Iran Radio, 29.1.77 reported that the illegality of work for women at night was discussed in the 'National Conference of Labour' and it was decided to nullify it. As the capitalist need of the cheap and efficient labour of women increases, the Shah follows suit and removes any obstacle against the entrance of women into the labour market.

you can imagine how terrible it would be to work under these conditions during the day!

And the law is absolutely silent about pay during maternity leave before and after the birth of the baby. Many women workers cannot afford to live without wages and there is no unemployment benefit.

There are many other points on which the law is silent. But let us juxtapose this labour law with the civil law which affects the status of women:

1. The law allows a man to forbid his wife any work interfering with the "benefit" or "dignity" of the family.
2. A woman is not allowed to leave the country without the consent of her father or husband.[19]

That means that women workers are not legally free to choose their own jobs. And let us assume - a very utopian assumption under the present repressive conditions in Iran - that a woman trade unionist is elected to represent her brothers and sisters abroad at an international labour conference. She might be unable to attend the conference if her husband or father does not permit her to go.

Now let us turn to the booklet entitled "The Rights of Women Workers" published by the Women's Organisation of Iran which is presided over by Princess Ashraf, twin sister of the Shah. On pages 6 and 8 it states:

> "The wages of women and men for equal work are equal...If the law is not carried out it is often due to lack of information... Most employers have kinder feelings towards their women workers (than towards their male employees) but they do not know all the details of the law so they do not put it into practice... Observation of all laws is beneficial to everybody, to the worker, the employer and all people."[20]

---

19. For further information see WORKERS OF IRAN, pp. 13-16.
20. In Persian, our translation.

در گذشته دستمزد زن کارگر ناچیز بود، و گاه یک زن نصف مزد یک
مردرا می گرفت درحالی که همان کار را انجام می داد. ولی امروز چنین نیست.

۵

The translation reads:

"In the past the wage of a women worker was negligible, and sometimes the woman received half the wages of a man whereas she did the same work. But TODAY it is not so."

This is an example of the systematic propaganda which the women workers in Iran are subjected to.

This booklet is written in very simple Persian language[21] and is designed for the consumption of working-class women. Even so, its assumptions of beneficient behaviour on the part of the employers who are busy cruelly exploiting these women sticks in our throats.

But reality sometimes creeps into even official publications of the WOI. Let us study a booklet written by an assistant professor at Tehran University, Dr. Zafardookht Ardalan, and called: "A Study and Analysis of Article 10 of the United Nations Declaration on the Elimination of Discrimination Against Women", published in 1975 by the Women's Organisation of Iran.

> "Equal wages for equal work which is article 23 of the Labour Law... is not put into practice in regard to most female workers...In this connection it has been shown that if the women workers are asked about their real wages they don't answer for fear of being dismissed by the employer."

---

21. Although the official language of Iran is Persian, all women workers are not Persians. There are other nationalities in Iran, such as Azarbaijanis, Arabs, Baluchis and Kurds, etc. Although there are no statistics about the numbers of the various nationalities in Iran, it is estimated that there are between 4-5 million Turki-speaking people, 2-3 million Arab speakers, 3-5 million Kurdish speakers and 1.5-2 million Baluchi speakers. The government has suppressed the social, cultural and economic rights and interests of all national minorities in Iran. This means that those women workers whose nationality is not Persian - and who anyway suffer greater hardships than their men because of the general attitude to women - must learn the official language, Persian, in order not only to read books like this but also for everyday life in their factories etc. The wages of national minority working women are lower compared with those of the Persians. For further aspects of the oppression of the Kurds in Iran see an excellent, informative booklet by A.R. Ghassemlou called Iranian Kurdistan, (no date, no publisher given). We shall mention in passing that in 1946 Azarbaijanis cntd. p. 29...

A KURDISH WOMAN.

And again:

> "...Most women workers in order to get an appropriate wage are forced to work 12 hours daily. Because they have left their children at home, and they are worried about them, as scientific research has shown, these mental worries are the cause of serious losses (i.e. breakages) in the workshop. (And according to article 41 a worker causing damage at work may have to pay for it.) This leads to dismissals."[22]

Dr. Ardalan also mentions article 19 which says that the employer is bound to give nursing mothers a half-hour break every 3 hours to suckle their babies. She adds that first, there is no guarantee that this will be carried out, and second, that the criterion for establishing nurseries should be the number of women workers as it is in countries such as Pakistan, etc., rather than the number of children as it is in Iran.

We would add that most carpet workshops, which are one of the main employers of women, are very small, so they are excused from this article. This means that even on paper they are deprived of this 'privilege' bestowed on them by His Imperial Majesty, the King of Kings!

Up to now we have used the concept of 'equality' without questioning how this 'equal' pay for equal work is determined. We know in this country that Babcock and Wilcox at Dumbarton,[23] in applying the concept of equality, interpreted it in a very unequal manner! Babcock and Wilcox in order not to pay the same wage for the same job to their male and female cleaners, designated male cleaners as "sanitary assistants" and paid them £1.17 per hour while paying £1.00 per hour to the female cleaners. One can imagine how the concept of equal pay for equal work is interpreted in Iran.

---

21. cntd... and Kurds established their own republic and both were able to converse officially in their own languages and women participated in elections and the running of their own administrative affairs. But the question of national minorities deserves a separate analysis.
22. Quoted in WORKERS OF IRAN, pp.18-19.
23. See Labour Research Volume 66, 3 March 1977, Equal Pay at the CAC.

Dr. Ardalan goes on to talk about the higher rate of illiteracy amongst women compared with men and how it affects them; because of it they have unequal job opportunities.

She says:

> "Women are mainly unskilled and to be skilled is exceptional and rare."

What is the government doing about this, to give equality of job training?

Dr. Ardalan says:

> "In this section (job training) it is absolutely certain that equality does not exist; of course we are talking about equality in practice, otherwise the law on training applies equally both to men and women." 24

(Our emphasis)

What about the problem of equal wages for equal work?

Dr. Ardalan again:

> "Most workshops are not willing to allow women to work under conditions of equality with men over wages and work; under equal conditions for men and women they would prefer to employ male workers."

Are there any loopholes through which the employer can avoid putting the labour law about women into practice? There is certainly one easy one. Dr. Ardalan talks about one of the prerequisites for benefiting from the labour laws being not to be a casual worker.

She says:

> "But some (read most of them: a better knowledge of the labour situation in Iran verifies this - T.J.) employers

---

24. All these quotations from Dr. Ardalan are from pp.29-30 of the Persian edition of her book.

misuse this prerequisite and employ women workers on a short-term basis."[25]

Dr. Ardalan also talks about the gross inequality of female representation in social activities (i.e. in the trade unions and co-operatives).[26]

Butthere are other questions which she does not raise, which we must. Up to now we have mainly dealt with the inadequacy or the silence of the laws on women, but we must raise questions about how the Iranian regime can provide evidence that these laws are put into practice.

1. Can those limited statistics on the number of women who are paid equal wages, backed with documentary evidence by which these figures can be verified, be produced?
2. What is the figure for pregnant women who were given unpaid leave and were later able to return to work?
3. How many nurseries are there and what are their locations?

In Britain the women workers who have been fighting for their rights know that it is they themselves who have won them; and that even after a century of struggle it was only by going on strike that the magnificent Trico women were able to force their employer to concede to equal pay, despite it being the law of the land. So it becomes very obvious that it is absurd to believe that decreed laws on women will be put into practice in a country like Iran without the support of a militant and organised women's labour movement.

4. WAGES AND SALARIES

A Chrysler trade unionist at an AEU branch meeting in Coventry very recently, said:

"I don't mind other workers, whether they are from Iran, South Africa or Chile, doing my work as long as they (the multinationals)

25. Ibid, p.32.
26. Ibid, p.30.

> pay them the same wages, and they work under the same conditions as I do."

Is the level of wages in Iran similar to that in Britain? The answer is a definite NO.

Who decides the level of wages in Iran, and how is the decision taken? Does free collective bargaining play any role in determining the level of wages?

Article 22 of the labour law mentions the minimum wage. We have already quoted in WORKERS OF IRAN (p.10) the French report in Le Monde Diplomatique atique of May 1975 which says that:

> "73% of the working population received an income below the statutory minimum living wage."

In Britain workers are protected from low wages in two ways: one, by legislation (Wages Councils Acts, etc.) and secondly, by free collective bargaining[27] which itself has an important effect on how the councils operate (and indeed these days the government is removing the councils in industries where unionism is strong). But in Iran, where 'free' collective bargaining does not exist, the minimum wage has a different meaning. The level of this minimum wage, or to put it more simply and correctly, the level of wages, is decided by a committee consisting of equal representatives of the employers, the government and the workers. In other words the government and the employers can always out-vote the workers' representative - of course assuming after a fierce struggle the workers have been able to elect their own true representative.

But how do they come to their decisions? The article states that they take into consideration the cost of living in the various parts of the country. But this raises further questions: are there reliable statistics which can be used to decide the cost of living? Although in practice reliable statistics are few and far

---

27. Before the introduction of the Social Contract which is contrary to the principle of "free" collective bargaining and which is against the interests of the working class.

    "Average take-home pay has now fallen to the level of 1971 when allowance is made for the increase in retail prices."

    Labour Research, March 1977, p.60.

between in Iran, let us assume for the sake of our argument that these exist. Does the committee take into account, for instance, the gap between the official prices of basic commodities and the prices which in practice the people have to pay to obtain these goods on the black market when they are in short supply, as they often are?

According to the latest government statistics[28], using the year beginning March 21, 1970 as the base 100, we can see how prices have risen:

Table 1:

Category of Expenses	1966	1975
Average	93.5	146.1
Foods	95.4	151.3
Clothing	97.3	145.6
Housing	84.2	164.1
Goods and services used at home	92.7	121.8
City and inter-city transport	93.9	114.4
Medical and hygienic expenses	90.4	126.6
Personal expenses	91.9	135.0
Other goods and services	99.4	122.1
Furniture	84.2	171.3

But there are plenty of examples which show these figures cannot be relied on. We have already quoted a terrible example of how rents are increased.[29] From discussions which we have had with a cross-section of workers and professional people from Iran, it is clear that government figures do not tell the full story. Instead of rents doubling, as the figures above would have you believe, they have in reality been increased anywhere from 6 to 12 times their original figure in the period 1966-75. Again, according to government statistics, the monthly

28. Yearly Statistics of March 1975, published in March 1976.

29. Page 8, WORKERS OF IRAN - see also Le Monde October 5, 1976.

housing expenses for an average Iranian family went down from 20.4% of their total expenses in 1971 to 15% in 1972 and only rose again to 19.2% in 1973 (no later figures available). But we have to remember that these figures take in everyone in Iran from those who receive £3,000 per month and pay out £1,000 on housing, to those nomads (3-5% of the population) who literally pay no rent because they live in the tents they make themselves - and therefore the statistics are meaningless. Almost every worker who lives and works in the larger cities where industrial complexes are located can testify that for them:

1. Rents did not come down in the years 1971-72;
2. the average monthly housing expenses of 2,110.9 rials (or 19.2% of the total expenses, 1972-73), according to the official statistics, are unrealistic and would not pay even for a decent room without basic facilities, let alone a home;
3. the figure given for total expenses (an average of 10,994.4 rials per month, 1972-73) exceeds the wages of 80-90% of workers in Iran who received about 4,500-6,000 rials per month in the same year.

Basic food prices have increased in actual life between two to four times during the period 1966-75 whereas the above figures put the rate at 1.58 times. Basic clothing such as underwear, stockings, suits, woollen jumpers (all of a good quality which will not wear out after a month or two) are more expensive in Tehran than in London. Generally clothes are much inferior in quality in Iran. Iranian visitors, who come mainly from rich families, in London swarm into Marks and Spencers to buy large amounts of clothing which is then sometimes resold to others in Iran. Another problem facing the workers is where to find the basic foods they need to keep up their health and strength for work: meat and factory-made butter, for instance, are often kept at the back of shops and sold only to known rich customers and then at a price chosen by the shopkeeper which is probably much above the official rate. Still another problem is the quality of the food - the price of milk in Tehran may be the same as that in London but the quality is completely different. Half a dozen small eggs cost 25-35p; apples about 30-50p per llb and boned veal from 80-£1.20p per llb; chicken is between 60-80p per llb. Butter, at 55-65p per llb is more on a par with England.

According to Kayhan ticket sellers and bus conductors in Tabriz are paid £1.33 (£1 = 120 rials) per day;

> "and according to their own words, under the present situation, this amount is the pocket money of a child of rich parents."[30]

The High Labour Council has set the minimum wage for March 1976-77 at between 141-152 rials in various regions whereas the minimum wage was 31-40 rials in 1946. In other words, in the last 30 years the minimum wage has increased 380%, 12.66% per year. Compare this with the oil revenue of $23 billion[31] in 1976 and the 1946 figure of only £7,130,250[32], i.e. roughly about 1897% increase or an annual increase of 63.2% - provided we use the present rate of exchange between dollars and pounds.

It seems all these low wages were not enough, and recently the Shah has said:

> "The Shahanshah has decreed the establishment of a high-powered Imperial Commission to prevent wastage of human and material resources, especially of agricultural and industrial products."[33]

(Our emphasis).

Later the Iranian Press reported that those workers who refused to work harder were being dismissed:

> "Several workers who hesitated or delayed to carry out their duties - (very hard work T.J.) were prevented to continue to work and were dismissed."[34]

The Shah has also said, complaining that workers don't work hard enough, that:

> "this is intolerable in contemporary Iran. Those who do not work, we shall take them by the tail and throw them out - like mice."[35]

---

30. Kayhan, May 19, 1976.
31. Shah: Kayhan International, October 25, 1976.
32. J. Amuzegar, M.A. Fekrat, Iran: 'Economic Development Under Dualistic Conditions', p.19., University of Chicago Press, 1971.
33. Kayhan International, November 9, 1976.
34. Tehran Economist, November 20, 1976.
35. Kayhan International, October 25, 1976.

Compare this extremely low (although by no means the lowest) wage with those paid to foreign workers. Again from Kayhan we learn that foreign workers pay very high rents in Iran:

> "...because the minimum rent is about 50,000 rials, (about £409.83) and the maximum rent exceeds 200,000 rials, (about £1,639.34) per month."[36]

A South Korean chemist said:

> "I am paid 140,000 rials (£1,147.5) per month in Iran. I cannot save any money because the cost of living is high. I was paid less at home in South Korea but I was able to save."[37]

Chan, another South Korean said:

> "I work in a shipbuilding company and I receive £2,000 monthly - I received one-third of this sum at home."[38]

> "But he complained about the high cost of living in Iran. He emphasized that in spite of his high salary he could save more at home although his salary was less than he now received. Kim, his friend, emphasized that rents in Iran were ten times higher than in South Korea."[39]

So we can see that even with the highest wages it is not easy to live in Iran - how much more must this be so for the Iranian worker who received very much less. Of course not all foreign employees receive such a high salary in Iran. There are many Afghan workers who are paid only 15,000 rials monthly (£122.95).

One important factor which shows the desperately low level of wages in Iran is the way in which workers will risk their lives to go on strike for better wages. We say risk their lives because strikers are imprisoned and tortured or shot down by soldiers for daring to make this protest.

---

36. Kayhan, October 16, 1976, - rate of exchange £1 = 122 rials.
37. Ibid.
38. Ibid.
39. Ibid.

In article 22 the words, "essential requirement" occur. But what does this employer-dominated committee see as "essential requirements"? Is a flat with a bathroom an essential requirement? How many calories does a worker in different occupations need daily? (And here we may say that according to FAO standards Iranian workers are undernourished).

Every British worker who has fought for his wages knows that you cannot leave the level of your wages to a bosses' committee. But let us now go on to ask, what happens in practice after the decisions on wages are made? We know that in Britain in 1969, for example, the wages of 271,000 workers were examined by inspectors and £171,000 in arrears were paid to 13,000 because of their actions.* But can the regime in Iran produce verifiable statistics on:

1. How many complaints from workers has the Ministry of Labour registered since the Law came into force?
2. How many workers were involved?
3. How many inspectors are working on checking the observation of article 22 by the employers?
4. How much money was paid back to the workers as a result of these complaints?
5. How many employers (and their names) were prosecuted for non-observation of this Law?

There is ample evidence that this sham minimum wage law is not observed and that government officials are being bribed by employers to close their eyes to this fact. The Pahlevi regime, which came from relative poverty to great riches itself, cannot stop corruption amongst its officials. According to information from an Iranian underground newspaper, sometimes as many as 78-82% of those complaints made to the Ministry of Labour about nonpayment of the minimum wage and other grievances are rejected because the complaints are said to be unfounded. And the remainder (18-22%) where the Ministry admits some grounds for complaints? There is no evidence that anything constructive is done about them. Even these figures are misleading in the sense that they do not take into account the following categories

---

* Quoted on p.210 of The Worker and the Law, K.W. Wedderburn, Pelican, 1971.

of workers who are very unlikely to complain at all:

1. An advanced sector of the working class who are concerned with the anti-working class nature of the Ministry of Labour and spends most of its time on underground organising instead of complaining to authorities;
2. That section of the workers which has recently moved into the towns from the countryside to find work at the factories. They very often do not know their rights and so do not usually complain;
3. Another section who might want to complain but would soon realise that their insistence on the right to complain must result in their being labelled as "subversives" and so endanger their jobs. They realise how difficult it is to get a job;
4. Another large section of the workers is purposely employed as casual labourers or workers for years on end at their place of work and this means that they are not covered by the legislation, and are not entitled to complain.

It is obvious that this matter of statutorily controlled wage agreements is a great barrier against the trade unionists who are striving to establish free collective bargaining in Iran - as the workers in Britain have lately begun to realise clearly. In 1950, under pressure from the labour movement, Mr Attlee could say:

> "The government has not at any time given direction as to the line which they should take to those who have the duty of arbitrating on claims, whether as members of the Industrial Court, the National Arbitration Tribunal or Wages Councils or as single arbitrators. To have done so would clearly have been to destroy the utility of this machinery."[40]

Various attempts have since been made in Britain, under both Labour and Tory governments, to control wages but once again the workers are beginning to realise that such control in the name of defeating inflation simply makes them worse off without destroying the underlying economic ills. An independent labour movement does not exist at the moment in Iran and the impetus for it is not

---

40. Quoted on p.227 of A History of British Trade Unionism, Henry Pelling, Pelican, 1973, - TUC 1950 Congress.

helped by the present control of wage bargaining - as the Donovan Report said about the conditions in England:

> "The Wages Council system could sometimes act not as a stimulant to collective bargaining but as a barrier to union recruitment and voluntary negotiation."[41]

Most British workers who are employed by multi-national companies, such as Leyland, Chrysler, Massey-Ferguson etc., should realise that their bargaining power can be strengthened by solidarity on an internation scale; and that low wages and a lack of independent trade unions in fascist countries can affect their own wages in this country.

Note 1 of article 21 makes provision for 'non-pecuniary' wages, i.e. wages in kind. The truck system of paying wages was the subject of one of the earliest and most bitter battles of the workers in the first half of the 19th century in Britain and was finally disposed of by an amending Act of 1887 to the original Act of 1831. That Iranian workers can still be paid in kind and not in proper money wages, or perhaps forced to buy goods and food (possibly at inflated prices) in their employers' shops is an indication of backwardness which should not be tolerated today - and we can safely predict that the Shah's regime in its eagerness to appear 'progressive' will not long tolerate this article in its labour law. But abolishing it on paper will not make it disappear in practice until the workers are strong enough to enforce this.

According to NALGO:

> "People's living standards depend not only on their pay cheque but on their social wage - education, health care, social services, pensions, and so on, paid for out of taxes."[42]

---

41. Quoted on p.211 of The Worker and the Law, K.W. Wedderburn, Pelican, 1971.
42. Quoted on p.85 of Book Two of Trade Union Studies, BBC, 1976.

To judge from this quotation there are many areas where the workers in Iran suffer: lack of proper health care, for instance, and social services and pensions. The regime spends billions of pounds (over £8 billion)[43] on the most sophisticated armaments and yet according to the latest apologist for the Shah, Margaret Laing, (who uses every trick to justify the Shah's brutality) there are only some 10,000 doctors - half of them in Tehran - for a population of 33 million.[44] Ms. Laing does not explain why thousands of Iranian doctors are practising in West Europe and the United States of America, and refusing to work in their own country, or why Iran with such a high oil revenue of around $23 billion (though recently the revenue has decreased due to OPEC policies) cannot spend more on training doctors instead of spending billions on arms.

5. DURATION OF WORK

Article 11 stipulates a 48 hour working week for the workers. But the same article mentions that there will be exceptions to this general rule. Note 2 of Article 12 also allows 4 hours overtime every day. Article 13 states that in the event of the occurence of an accident the worker must work for the employer if he is asked to do so. This all means that on top of 48 hours normal work the worker can do 24 hours overtime which makes a working week of 72 hours. Making overtime on certain conditions compulsory deprives the worker of the right to say whether he will work overtime or not.

Remembering the gap between actual wages and the real cost of living, and also that there is a well-armed police force to break up any resistance from the workers, one can have a good idea of how many hours the workers really do work. A minimum of 10 to 12 hours per day is common practice.[45]

---

43. The Financial Times, August 9, 1976, gives the figure of $10 billion.
44. The Shah, Margaret Laing, Sidgwick & Jackson, 1977, p.224.
45. See pp. 11-12 WORKERS OF IRAN. In Iran, because of low wages when workers'overtime is reduced they have to go on strike. In May 1976, about 4,000 miners in a coal mine near Shahrud which is located in the North of Iran near the Caspian Sea went on strike. One of the causes of the strike was that the employers had reduced the overtime hours. The mine

cntd...

Apologists of the Pahlevi regime (like Margaret Laing in her book on The Shah and Woodrow Wyatt in his review of it [46]) having been confronted with the contradictory labour laws and the intense exploitation of the workers, came up with the argument that although it is true that the Shah violates all the basic human rights and has many similarities to Hitler still Germany was not a backward country like Iran and the Shah is the only one who can drag it into the 20th century and introduce the necessary changes. But what has actually happened?

The start of modern manufacturing firms early in this century and the concentration of the workers in these activities, the inflow of Iranian workers who had worked abroad and gained experience and knowledge of organising workers to defend their rights and interests, led to certain developments. At that time up to 1918 there was not a defined working day and the employers could make their workers work as long as they wished, 12 to 14 hours being normal. In that year, the printers were inspired by their fellow-workers in neighbouring countries who were fighting for workers' democracy, and they decided that they could no longer endure the long working day. They came together and discussed their grievances and put their demands to the employers who promptly threatened them with government prosecution, and the workers saw how the government supported the employers. The workers, faced with constant harassment by the police, organised a strike; the printing union provided the necessary guidance, and it took 14 days to make the employers accept the workers' demands.[47]

---

45. cntd... area was surrounded by the army and the combined forces of army and SAVAK had to give in and accept the workers' demands. One report indicates that many workers were arrested after the strike and were sent to be tortured in Semnan and Damaghan prisons.

46. Sunday Times, February 27, 1977.

47. Please see Appendix III for the text of a contemporary document, by M. Dehghan on Iranian Trade Unionists, on this struggle.

Since the history of the Iranian working class has been falsified (usually because the "historians" were not concerned about the history of "little men", as the Cambridge historian, Charles Kingsley, calls ordinary people), we have a duty to put the matter straight. These "little men" have an unregistered record of fighting for democracy, liberty and justice.

We have told you about the printers and the spread of trade unionism; now we wish to recount the case of the carpet weavers of Kerman.

In 1923 the carpet weavers of Kerman, among whom a large percentage were illiterate[48] women and children, fed up with their very long hours of work - usually 12-14 but in summer often 16 hours from sunrise to sunset - got together to protest. At this time in Iranian history there was no centralised police, no organised secret police, and the Prime Minister (Reza Khan, later to make himself King, and the father of the present Shah) was busy routing out his opponents in Tehran and could not send troops to shoot down the workers.[49] The carpet weavers' strike was so effective that the Governor-General of Kerman was forced to make the eight-hour day, and other demands of the workers, official by decree. And fortunately, this decree was sent to the ILO and since the text has survived we have a 'document' to prove our point and please the "respectable" historians.

(a) DOCUMENT

INTERNATIONAL LABOUR OFFICE

(Geneva, Switzerland)

Legislative Series, 1923 - Pers.1

PERSIA

(Kerman and Beluchistan)

PROTECTION OF WORKERS IN CARPET FACTORIES[50]

---

48. Some Iranian Professors should familiarise themselves with the struggle of these illiterate women and children and this might help them to correct their illusions that only educated people fight. They should also study how illiterate women and children organised successfully the Paris Commune affairs.
49. Even Peter Avery in his book, Modern Iran (p.211) concedes that Iran was broken up into regions with each its own ruler at that time.
50. The Persian text received by the ILO has no title.

(Decree of the Governor-General (Wali) of Kerman and Beluchistan respecting the protection of workers in carpet factories.)

Date: December 17, 1923 (25 gows (sic) 1302.

In view of the necessity for due regard to hygiene and the improvement of the conditions of employment of workers in carpet factories and for the observance of the precepts and commands of the Holy Religion of Islam, which the government and His Excellency the Sardar Sepah, Prime Minister, Minister of War and Commander-in-Chief of the military force of the Persian Empire (may his name live forever) have always in mind, the following regulations are hereby issued:

1. The working day of all workers in carpet factories shall be eight hours. The manufacturers (employers) shall not be entitled to require their workers to work longer than the specified hours.

2. On Fridays and Public Holdiays work shall be suspended in all carpet factories, and the workers shall be entitled to receive their wages for those days as for working days.

3. Boys under eight years of age and girls under ten years of age shall not be employed in these factories.

4. The boys' workshop shall be separate from the girls' workshop.

5. In the girls' workshop women shall be employed as forewomen (persons who dictate the patterns to the workers) and the employment of foremen in the girls' workshops shall be absolutely prohibited.

6. A manufacturer shall not in any case engage or retain a worker suffering from a contagious disease.

7. Carpet workshops shall have windows toward the south, so that the sun can enter them.

8. The carpet weaving looms shall be 1 metre above the floor of the workshop and the seat shall be high enough for the children to be able to perform their work comfortably.

9. The head of the Public Health Service or the municipal medical officer shall visit and inspect each factory every month. If the prescribed sanitary and hygienic requirements are not complied with, he shall report the matter to the competent quthority, which shall at once take action.

10. A fine of not less than 10 and not more than 50 tomans , which shall be allocated to the Department of Education for maintenance of the schools, or imprisonment for not less than 1 day and not more than 20 days, shall be imposed for every contravention of the provisions of the preceding sections.

11. The Police Department shall be responsible for supervising the carrying out of these provisions and for seeing that they are not contravened.

But recently a "trade unionist" called Mr. R. Joorabchi (who is the General Secretary of the Executive Board of the syndicate of workers at Donyaye Felez - (Metal Universe) at a meeting organised to celebrate the 50 years of the Pahlevi regime, and where the workers were expected to express their deep gratitude for all the "benefits" bestowed on them by the Shah, spoke of this document. He said:

> "In the ILO magazine there is a decree <u>from</u> the Sardar Shah (Commander-in-Chief) Prime Minister, Minister of War <u>to</u> the Governor-General of Kerman and Baluchistan about welfare and hygiene, and the working hours of the carpet weavers".[51]
>
> (Our emphasis)

According to another paper[52] the same speaker went on to say:

> "The text of this document indicates that at those times when the workers of recently industrialised countries of the world were fighting and striking against their employers <u>for shorter working hours</u> and better welfare conditions,the learned leader of Iran, His Imperial Majesty Reza Shah,the Great, <u>with one decree reduced the working hours to 8</u> and issued the decree for the welfare and hygiene of the workers."
>
> (Our emphasis)

---

51. Ettelaat, Thursday, July 8, 1976

52. Kayan, Thursday, July 8, 1976

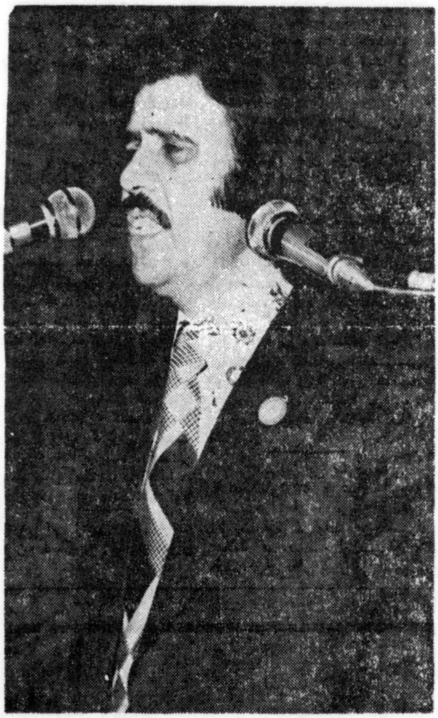

آقای رضا جورابچی نماینده کارگران دنیای فلز

Mr. Reza Joorabchi the "representative" of workers at Donyaye Felez who falsifies the Labour Movement history so that he can defend the Shah.

In the first place the text that Mr. Joorabchi was referring to must be seen within the following points:

1. Mr. Joorabchi's claim that the decree was issued by Reza Khan (not yet Shah) is absolutely false. The decree was issued by the Governor-General of Kerman and the law is operative only in the province of Kerman.

Before Reza Khan became King in 1925 there was no central government and no complete centralised legislative bodies, i.e. on the provincial level the Governor-General would rule like a king and would issue decrees.

Even Mr. P. Avery, the apologist for the Pahlavi dynasty, corroborates this point:

> " This situation could be compared to the rise of muluku't-tavayif, literary, sectional or regional kings, a recurring phenomenon of Persian history whenever central government was ineffective. In other words when Reza Shah seized power, the Iranian Empire was fragmented..." [53]

2. The decree has very strong religious undertones and mentions the name of Reza Khan only as someone who observes "the precepts and commands of the Holy Religion of Islam". We should remember that Reza Khan forced at bayonet point Muslim women to remove their veils ("Reza Shah..... prohibited the use of the veil by women .....") [54]

3. The ILO has received the text from the Iranian Government and without checking the truthfulness of it has printed it as it was. On the other hand if one looks at some of the present ILO documents, such as Employment and Incomes Policy in Iran, one can see how an ILO mission can be deceived by the government propaganda into repeating the same lies that the regime tells.

---

53. P. Avery, Modern Iran, p.221

54. A. Bausani, The Persians, p. 177

4. At this time there was a nationwide trade union movement and the carpet weavers had a trade union and they struggled for their rights. Mr. Joorabchi is a typical example of the calibre of the "trade unionist" or "worker's representative" who defends the Shah and is a representative of that trend in the present regime of Iran which wants to falsify the history of the Iranian labour movement in the following ways:

1. To omit the names and struggles of those trade unionists and workers who fought heroically against the employers and the government which represented the interests of the employers.

2. To prevent the spread of the news of the present struggle, strikes, sit-ins, demonstrations.

3. In the case, historically recorded, of those battles in which the Labour Movement has forced the Pahlavi dynasty to concede their demands, they are represented as the favours given by the King of Kings to the workers. They are forging texts and documents to support their claims.

4. The regime employs mercenary historians who are expert in finding "documents" i.e. those written texts which are written under the police surveillance of the Kings to provide a prop for the present system.

6. INDUSTRIAL SAFETY AND OCCUPATIONAL HEALTH

According to Article 47 a High Safety Council draws up and approves "regulations providing for occupational health and workers' safety".

This High Safety Council consists of six government ministers or under-secretaries plus the Master of the Engineering College of Tehran University; (no workers, or even employers, are thought fit to sit on the highest body). Article 49 requires such approval for new tools.

Article 50 allows for the closure of unsafe working places on the recommendation of the Labour Inspector to the Public Investigator and with the consent of the Ministry of Labour. It would be interesting to know how many times such a closure has been carried out, particularly against a multi-national company. The Iranian Government, and the Shah, are in power by courtesy of the CIA and the multi-nationals which flocked to Iran in the wake of the coup of 1953, and we know of no significant case in which the state has acted against the interests of multi-nationals.

We would like to ask the following questions:

Can the government provide reliable statistics on:

1. How many of the existing working places pass the safety standards of the High Safety Council? (Apart, of course, from those few model workplaces which are shown to foreign journalists and visitors. We know of specific examples where SAVAK agents have ordered employers to build modernised workshops because the government wanted to make a film of it for propaganda purposes).

2. How many Labour Inspectors are there, and what are their qualifications?

3. How often are all workshops inspected?

4. Is there any written record of the reports of the Inspectorate? If so, where are they kept and who has access to them?

5. How many workshops lack basic facilities like toilets and bathrooms?

6. Has there ever been any investigation of possible corruption of labour inspectors (and other officials) by the employers? Such cases are well known to exist, and this is not surprising in a country where the graft system starts at the top. The Inspectors may even be paying bribes to their superiors.

7. LABOUR INSPECTION

Article 52 gives labour inspectors the right to enter all the working places covered by the Act at any time to carry out their inspections. This sounds very interesting, until we ask some questions such as; how often do they exercise that right (and we note that methods of inspection are covered by unspecified special regulations); and we further ask; what is the relationship between the labour inspectors and the secret police?

Can the government guarantee that these inspectors do not pass on information about the workers to SAVAK - of course this is an absurd question for those who know that the secret police tries to pervade every section of society and that there are no pratical barriers to them.

Article 53 states that labour inspectors have no right, even after leaving their jobs, to divulge any commercial and technical secrets they may have learned in the course of their work. But what authority will decide what information is "commercial and technical" and what about the unsafe conditions under which workers do their jobs and risk their lives in order to earn a living? There are examples of labour inspectors being dismissed because they were thought to be unreliable about keeping commercial and technical secrets; but what they had really done was to divulge information to the "unauthorised" about the unsafe conditions of the working places! As can be seen, the conditions of the working places is a top secret in Iran and should not be allowed to fall into the hands of "subversives" and "foreign enemies" because that might endanger the security of the state!!

8. OFFENCES AND PENALTIES

Article 9 stated that:

> "employers are bound to prepare, and submit, in accordance with the relevant regulations, all statistics and data required by the Ministry of Labour".

Well, it is clear that these statistics are vital; but Article 57 shows how the Shah's regime is generous and subservient towards the employer. This article states that those employers who violate Article 9 will be liable to payment of a fine of 500-5,000 rials - about £4.16 - £41.60 [55]. The reader will remember that if a labour inspector divulges commercial and technical information he will be liable to a criminal prosecution under Article 220 of the Penal Code; but a

---

55. Rate of exchange: £1 = 119-121 rials

millionaire employer, for withholding information wanted by the government on wages and conditions of work, will be fined between £4.16 and £41.60.'

Article 58 states that if an employer violates Article 11 (8 hours working day); Article 12 (rates for overtime); Article 14 (Friday to be rest day); Article 15 (official holidays); Articles 21-23 (wages and salaries) - the employer will be fined between 1,000 and 10,000 rials (£8.32 to £83.20). The Article says that the maximum fine should apply to employers assigning overtime to children under 16.

Article 10 carries the same penalties with one to two months' imprisonment in addition and the maximum penalty goes to those employing children under 12.

Article 61 is extremely fascinating. It states:

> "Any person who by force and threat or by using coercion compels another to accept membership of a syndicate and or keeps him from joining a syndicate, shall be liable to payment of a fine of 1,000 to 10,000 rials, or a term of correctional imprisonment ranging from one month to two months or to both punishments."

Article 63 states that the fines referred to shall be paid into a "special account" in a bank.

Can the regime produce any reliable figures about how much money has been paid into this account, the names of the employers concerned, and where and how this money has been spent? If yes, how much has the Shah paid into this account?'.

The final Article, No. 69 states that the Ministry of Labour and the Ministry of Justice are charged with carrying out and enforcing the provisions of the Act.

There is enough experience in Britain (the recent judgements against the proposed Post Office Workers' strike in London and in Scotland, Lord Cameron's injunction against NALGO leaders preventing them holding a strike) for workers to know the anti-working class bias of judges - as well as government officials.

9. CONCLUSIONS

1. The present labour law violates the most basic democratic rights and in some respects is worse than fascist Franco;

2. The law is unequal; it is biased even on paper in favour of the employer;

3. The government is given extensive power to interfere in the workers' affairs;

4. In order to see whether anything at all in it is ever carried out one must have reliable statistics, and the Iranian regime cannot produce such statistics- again and again we must emphasize the word "reliable" because such a regime can produce any "document " it wishes.

The present labour law in Iran, like South Africa, is a direct consequence of the domination of the Iranian economy by International Capital. The only way that all this is going to be changed is through the struggles of the working class for free and democratic organisations. Of course this can be achieved only after the socio-economic rule of the present regime is overthrown and the working class seize political power.

Some of the foreign workers in Iran.

ATTEMPTS TO CONTROL THE LABOUR MOVEMENT

1. SAVAK

...سان

صفحه ٥
شنبه ١٤ اسفند ٢٥٣٥
٥ مارس ١٩٧٧ - شماره ١٠١٠٧

مصاحبه شاهنشاه با روزنامه «کریسچن ساینس مانیتور»

...اهنشاه: در ایران یک دقیقه
...عتصاب کارگری وجود ندارد

شاهنشاه تصریح فرمودند مشکلات اقتصادی غرب ناشی از فقدان انضباط واراده در کارکردن است در حالیکه در ایران یك دقیقه اعتصاب کارگری وجود ندارد.

THE SHAH - "IN IRAN THERE IS NOT ONE MINUTE OF WORKERS'STRIKES" [56]

Text on photo:

"The Shah - made it explicit that the difficulties of the West are due to lack of discipline and the way the work is managed; whereas in Iran there is not one minute of workers' strikes......" [57]

For footnotes, see next page

Is it true that there are such "wonderful" peaceful industrial relations in Iran? If yes, how has the Shah managed to achieve such "wonders"?

First, it is not true:

> "..... strikes (which are illegal) have begun to occur when in the past three months the Government has ineffectively sought to implement a wages policy." [58]

And workers fight for higher wages "..... after using the strike as a weapon".[59] We will return to the question of strikes later in the next part. But it is true that the Shah has managed to make life difficult for those workers who go on strike. One of the means which the Shah uses is "SAVAK", his secret police.

What is SAVAK?

It is the State Security and Intelligence Organisation created in 1957 and lead today by General Nassiri (an old schoolmate of the Shah, at the Military Academy) who has the formal title of Deputy Premier. In practice the head of SAVAK is in fact always appointed by the Shah and he is responsible to the Shah alone. This means that there is no limit - unless the Shah places one - on what SAVAK does and the methods it uses.

SAVAK defines its own aim as working

> "for the purpose of the security of the country and the prevention of any kind of conspiracy detrimental to public interests". [60]

---

56. Kayhan, March 5, 1977 - a response, perhaps - and a little late - to CRTURI's statement of March 5, 1976 that workers in Iran were being machine-gunned for striking and staging protests!
57. Ibid
58. Financial Times, June 21, 1976
59. Le Monde, October 5, 1976
60. Amnesty International, IRAN, November 1976 Briefing

SAVAK has an official budget which is stated openly: the true, hidden, figure at a conservative estimate is around £1 billion. Another secret is the number of its employees, active agents and administrative assistants, but again an estimate would put the figure at about 60,000 or more. This does not, of course, include secret informers!

A former head of SAVAK, General T. Bakhtiyar, has spoken about the global operations of SAVAK:

> "It is natural that SAVAK co-operates with the espionage organisations of friendly countries." [61]

Recently, a BBC T.V. reporter asked the Shah:

R: "You said that SAVAK's job is to keep an eye on Iranians both in this country and abroad and that they operate in the United States. Does SAVAK operate in Britain?"

S: "Yes, within the law, obviously, of your country. We know of your intelligence people in this country too. What are they doing here? They have a job to do".

R: " But what does SAVAK do in Britain?"

S: " Probably look at the circles or the organisations who are working against the interests of my country."

R: " Does it work with the co-operation of British intelligence?"

S: " Not in that sense no. It has an exchange of information with your intelligence, but not in that sense."

R: " You exchange information with British intelligence?"

S: " Yes, but this is on a much higher level". [62]

---

61. German weekly magazine, Der Spiegel, No. 43, 1967
62. KAYHAN International December 18, 1976

SAVAK agents are littered throughout the world often disguised with diplomatic titles and working from Iranian embassies.[63]

SAVAK in many respects, in terms of ruthlessness and brutality, is like DINA (the Chilean secret police) and BOSS (the South African one). Like them and in terms of using dirty tricks, like the CIA (its creators), it uses the most up-to-date methods, both physical and psychological. Like them, it operates on an international scale; and subjects the opponents of the regime to the most savage tortures. In terms of using brutal methods against individuals it has surpassed Hitler's Gestapo. We could continue this list of international similarities because all these forces are a direct consequence of similar modes of production which spawn them.[64] But there are differences between the modes of production of these three countries,[65] Chile, South Africa and Iran, which makes SAVAK have its specific characteristics.

---

63. See Sunday Times, May 12, 1974. The Guardian and The Times, July 23, 1976. The Sunday Times August 1, 1976. There was a programme about the collaboration between the West German Intelligence Service and SAVAK. Panorama, March 21, 1977, 8.15 p.m. Channel 1, West German Television.

64. Most left groups have correctly seen the similarities to Chile, etc. e.g.
    1. Being a sworn enemy of the working class;
    2. Using brutal methods to suppress opponents;
    3. All this done to create a heaven for investment by the multinationals - but no single group has acted systematically, despite excellent attempts, and from a materialist point of view, to explain the totality of the state of Iran.

65. This is a very complicated subject which deserves treatment on its own. And we know of no existence of a materialist analysis of the

(Continued)

Better understanding of SAVAK requires a more correct analysis of the Shah's capitalist state, which exhibits simultaneously the most advanced technological features of international capitalism and ancient pre-capitalist techniques and relationships of production.

Like Chile, the Shah's regime has been brought into power by the forces of international capital and through their watchdog, the CIA. At the present time the Iranian economy, like that of South Africa, is under the direct domination of multi-national companies which produce about 60-70 per cent, on estimate, of the GNP (which amounted to $47 billion for the year March 1975 to March 1976. Less than half of this GNP, about $23 billion was produced by the great oil cartels, Shell BP, Standard, etc.) but unlike the leaders of all these other countries, the Shah personally is one of the richest persons in the world and has investments throughout the world and is personally a co-partner of international capital. He can, and does, use this wealth to spend millions of pounds in the western universities and United Nations agencies so that this or that UN personality or academic can produce "theories" about his state and his policies and justify his crimes against the working people; and contrary to some views he has managed to make some inroads into these institutions.

As Shakespeare - in Timon of Athens - said:

> "Gold, yellow, glittering, precious gold!
> Thus much of this, will make black, white; foul, fair;
> Wrong, right; base, noble; old, young; coward valiant.
> ...Will lug your priests and servants from your sides;
> Pluck stout men's pillows from below their heads;

---

65. Cntd... totality of Iranian economy. We can only point here to the situation in Iran where the economic picture is complicated by, for instance, the use which the Shah makes of his immense wealth through the Pahlevi Foundation, the role of oil within the economy, and the relationship between the private and public sectors.

This yellow slave
Will knit and break religions; bless the accurs'd;
Make the hoar leprosy ador'd; place thieves,
And give them title, knee and approbation,
With senators on the bench."[66]

But the Shah lacks a purely capitalist profit-making world outlook. The Shah's world outlook is dominated by the pre-capitalist ideology mode of production although here and there you find glimpses of the most advanced capitalist ideas. His attitude to women is an excellent example of this.

The Iranian society is a newly developed capitalist economy which is partially industrialised and yet the Shah's form of state - both the government and the repressive state institutions such as SAVAK, etc. - has no resemblance to a 'classical' form of capitalist state and it is anachronistic. The Shah's state is different from, let us say, Britain, in this sense, that in Iran there is no separation of the judicial, executive and legislative aspects of the various institutions of the state such as the cabinet, the parliament, the secret police, the ordinary police, the courts: all of these are responsible to one single person, the Shah, who rules by decree and whose rubber-stamp parliament must approve all that he decrees. It is true that the Shah represents the interests of the capitalist and land-owning classes and the Shah himself belongs to these classes.

---

66. Quoted in K. Marx. Capital Volume One, Lawrence & Wishart, London, 1974, p.132.

One of the contrasts in Iran: the new steel mill at Esfahan - and a 3,000 year-old method of digging an underground irrigation system.

But the Shah does not always necessarily and consistently and persistently defend and respect the rights and interest and properties of the capitalist class. There are examples - although it is true that they are only a handful - where he has ordered the confiscation of the property of a capitalist or where he has curtailed their freedom of investment and to make profits.

The Shah and SAVAK, cannot only be explained in terms of objective conditions, forgetting the anti-working class ideas and theories. Looking at the Shah in this context we can see that he is on the one hand a representative of these classes and yet on the other hand acts in some limited respects independently of them. In this way he resembles Louis Bonaparte in 19th century France.[67]

SAVAK seen within the above context can clearly be shown to have similarities to, and differences from, other secret police organisations like DINA, BOSS, etc. But the task of a materialist, historical approach is incomplete and insufficient without stating the specific historical characteristics of a single phenomenon.

SAVAK differs from other agencies in the following main ways:

1. SAVAK is responsible to one single individual only, the Shah.
2. SAVAK has, through the personal riches of the Shah and through the oil revenue accruing to the government, unspecified funds at its disposal.
3. SAVAK has no practical limitations on its activities[68] and can literally do anything provided the Shah approves of it.

---

67. By no means do we want to state that the Shah's regime is a Bonapartist regime; the Shah's regime is one hundred times more brutal than Bonaparte's, and differs in many other respects.

68. See, for the British secret police, Tony Bunyan's "The Political Police in Britain", (Quartet Books, 1977) for the similarities and contrasts of what happens here.

All these advantages make SAVAK one of the most efficient secret police forces in the world. But SAVAK in relation to the struggle of the workers and the fight of the workers, is inefficient and ineffective. The Shah's statement that there exists not "one minute's strike' is just a wishful whim which will never come true under the present mode of production. This statement only reflects the inner fear of this "almighty ruler" of what workers can do when united.

The brutality and ruthlessness of SAVAK is only one part of the reality and one side of the truth; and could be extremely harmful to the labour movement if it is not combined with the other part of the story which is the successful underground struggle of various groups against the regime in Iran and the continuous strikes of the workers. One should remember that SAVAK is different from the CIA in this sense, that the CIA tries in every possible way to cover up its activities - not always, fortunately, very successfully! But SAVAK only tries to hide some aspects of its activities (the brutalities and deaths, and the CIA involvement in the labour movement)[69] and on the contrary, tries to magnify and propagate the idea of its strength and all-powerfulness, as the Gestapo did, in order to secure blind obedience.

The CIA in many respects has violated the American constitution and is now frightened of "public opinion" and reaction,[70] but SAVAK recognises no law and is apparently worried about no "public opinion" or reaction inside Iran.[71]

---

69. A very important aspect that still many Iranian opposition groups have not yet exposed effectively!

70. We are conscious that the concept "public opinion" is very vague, and usually manipulated by the capitalist mass media.

71. But the Shah responds very differently to international public opinion outside Iran and that is one of the reasons he spends millions to deceive them.

SAVAK makes every attempt to propagate the idea that every slight movement against the Shah and his government will be detected and stopped by SAVAK. It is not true in the first place that SAVAK eyes and ears are everywhere; and secondly it has been proved by experience that most SAVAK agents are so inefficient (and do the job usually for mercenary rather than ideological reasons) that it is possible for an underground movement to be organised and to function both within Iran and abroad.

Therefore the passage in the American weekly Newsweek:[72]

> "By almost any conceivable measure, the size and scope of SAVAK operations are absolutely staggering. Between 30,000 and 60,000 people work for SAVAK full time, but they are only the skeleton of a much larger creature. According to some diplomats in Iran no fewer than 3 million Iranians - one out of eight adult citizens - are occasional SAVAK informers. As a result the agency's eyes and ears are everywhere: in hotels, taxis, schools, foreign embassies and companies, factories, doctor's offices, even in the dormitories and cafetarias where Iranian students live and eat while studying abroad..."

can be seen on the one hand as an expression of the desire of SAVAK to dominate Iranian life and on the other hand as a propaganda exercise in carrying out this desire. Even organisations like CBS TV of the United States, which may believe that they are conducting an impartial investigation into SAVAK can be used to bolster up the Shah and his regime and to give a very distorted picture of the secret police.[73]

---

72. October, 1974.

73. One of their employees recently asked us to give face-to-face interviews regarding our policies and experiences (CBS letter dated February 2, 1977 to the CRTURI) but because of the lack of proper safeguards, and because we had some doubts about the way CBS was going to represent SAVAK, we could not consent to take part in such a programme without certain conditions. We wrote a letter dated February 8, 1977, and stipulated our conditions.

Such statements as this:

> "Everything I had said during my stay in the U.S. in the academic year of 1972-1973, before my imprisonment, had been reported to SAVAK, which operates on a global scale." [74]

do not in the slightest way vindicate the efficiency of SAVAK. Why? Because SAVAK could have employed the most moronic person and given him an efficient tape recorder, and instructed him to record the professor in class.

SAVAK efficiency has to be seen within the context of its operation against those who are fighting underground to overthrow the regime of the Shah. There is unquestionable evidence thatthere are underground organisations operating in Iran. There is also evidence that neither has SAVAK been able to stop workers' and students' strikes in Iran in the past nor will it be able to do so in the future.

And then, take this statement:

> "In the case of the women, the electric baton is moved over the naked body with the power increased on the breasts and interstices of the vagina. I have heard women screaming and laughing hysterically, shouting, Dont do it, I'll tell you." (Our emphasis.)

The first part of the paragraph describes accurately the savage methods SAVAK uses against women who are fighting against injustice; but fortunately there are examples where women have been subjected to exactly the same brutal torture if not more so and they have not said,

> "Don't do it, I'll tell you."

If torture always yielded such results then there would be little prospect of fighting international capital.

---

74. Terror in Iran by R. Baraheni. The New York Review October 28, 1976.

75. Ibid. R. Baraheni. It is true that SAVAK operates on a global scale; see The Sunday Times, August 1, 1976 - C.R.T.U.R.I. is also one of the targets of SAVAK in this country.

Houshang Targool, a worker executed in October 1971 after being "tried" by a Military tribunal for the "crime" of distributing Marxist literature, said to his accusers:

> "In these crucial moments I bid farewell to life with infinite joy and hopeful of tomorrow's success. Yes, I am leaving life. Not because I have had enough of life; but because life achieved at the expense of others' nobility and lives is base. In my opinion death is a thousand times sweeter than such a life."

The examples of political detainees in Algeria,[76] in Vietnam, and also various examples in Iran, have proved that men and women, and even children, can survive any torture provided that they are determined and are deeply convinced of their beliefs and ideas.[77]

On an international scale it has been proved that the most brutal and efficient secret police cannot destroy the determination of those who fight against international capital.

---

76. See F. Fan on, Dying Colonialism, for the effect of torture on political prisoners, and how they can resist it.

77. F. Tonekaboni, in, The First Strike, written in Persian and later translated into German in, Feuer unterm Pfauenthron, (edited by B. Nirumand Rotbuch Verlag, Berlin, 1974), tells the story of a worker called Kaveh, caught and tortured by SAVAK for speaking out as a worker's representative (and offered his freedom if he would become a SAVAK spy). Kaveh replies to his torturers:
"I've earned my living myself since I was five years old. If I couldn't work in a factory I would go as a labourer on a building site. And if that wasn't possible, I'd go stealing. And if I didn't have the courage for that, I'd become a pimp. But what you suggest, I never can and will do it."
This fictional account, Tonekaboni wrote, we are told by his friends, after questioning many workers about their experiences. He himself has now been imprisoned by the Shah - because of his writings.

Recent apologists for the regime have been under pressure from world 'public opinion' to admit the Shah's brutality, but nevertheless they justify his actions on the grounds that the majority of people in Iran are illiterate and the Shah only uses force in order to move these illiterate [78] people and to improve their standard of living.

It is vital and essential to counteract this lie about the working people of Iran; we have to publicise as much as possible the great determination of those working people who are fighting for better wages, conditions and relations of work.

It is also necessary to examine with some care what is said by those who take part in the struggle against the Shah and seek to expose SAVAK activities. For instance, most existing books or articles on SAVAK, either by Iranian opposition groups, or by Western journalists, are either completely silent on the question of SAVAK (and CIA) involvement in operations against the labour movement, or deal with it in a very sketchy manner.

The Tudeh Party of Iran -counterpart of British C.P. - has published, in English, a pamphlet on SAVAK [79] which has hardly one word on SAVAK operations in the labour movement; and the same can be said for two Persian language books produced by the Confederation of Iranian Students (National Union).[80]

---

78. These apologists should be reminded of this historical fact:
"...As a result of this organisation, 45, of the 700 women who assembled at the All-Russian Women's Congress in 1908 were socialists, 30 of these 45 factory workers, some still scarcely able to read."
From Sheila Rowbotham's introduction to Women Workers' Struggle for Their Rights by Alexandra Kollontai published by Falling Wall Press, March 1973. Also of the illiterate Kerman women and children Carpet Weavers in 1923.

79. SAVAK - Shah's Secret Police Published by Central Committee of Tudeh-Party, no date of publication is given. Probably 1974 or 1975. pp 18.

80. see next page.

In "On SAVAK" we read:

> "The suppression of the workers and peasants is the main task of SAVAK"[81]

but the book does not go into details of <u>how</u> SAVAK is tackling this task, and deals in an extremely sketchy manner with the CIA role in the Iran labour movement.

The "Documents on SAVAK" hardly mention the SAVAK operation in the labour movement. Parviz Khonsari, officially known as the head of Student and Cultural and Social Affairs Abroad - and one of SAVAK's leading disguised agents! - is mentioned in this role[82] but not as Iran's permanent representative at ILO.[83] It is clear from a survey which we have made of the literature on the situation in present-day Iran, covering not only all kinds of opposition groups with a very wide range of political spectrum but also more general reportage by journalists and others, that the question of SAVAK, and CIA, operations in the labour movement has been neglected completely.

Let us repeat what SAVAK supposedly works for:

> "the security of the country and the prevention of any kind of conspiracy detrimental to public interests."

What do these words mean? They should read:

> "the security of international capital and the prevention of any kind of struggle which is detrimental to the interestsof international capital."

It should be remembered that SAVAK was created in the period of reaction following the 1953 coup, and after the 1941-1953 era when the labour movement showed that it could organise itself and in fact became a force to be reckoned with.

---

80. "On SAVAK" published December 1969, "Document On SAVAK" December 1976 both published by CISNU - it must however be added that these two books are important works - in spite of their defects.
81. P.17. Our translation.
82. P.10. Document On SAVAK.
83. The supervision of executing this contract (training of Iranian workers'..cntd...

This was particularly so amongst the oil workers[84], and this was seen as an immediate and dangerous blow being struck at international capital.

The penetration of international capital and the extension and deepening of repression in Iranian society are two sides of the same coin, and only those with double standards can doubt this. Too many examples occur in our world - Chile, South Africa, Brazil, Iran, Argentina, just to give a few examples.

But international capitalism does not repress every class in a given society: It becomes co-partner of indigenous capitalists, seeks out allies amongst professional people, and the workers become the prime target of this repression. In Iran it directs its repression against the labour movement both openly, through laws and through SAVAK and, secretly, through covert CIA operations.

Why has the issue of this extremely harmful SAVAK -and CIA - operation against the Iranian labour movement been neglected?

The answer is not a simple one, but we can say this much; bourgeois theorists have misled some groups into underestimating the potentiality and the actual strength of the labour movement in Iran. This underestimation has been reinforced by the lack of easily accessible documents on the actual struggles, both past and present (except those falsified by the regime).

These two propositions can form a vicious circle and it is necessary for us to break out of it. We can do this by starting an abstract debate on the potential and actual strength and consciousness of the labour movement; or we can begin to

---

83. cntd... "representatives" at Turin ILO Training Center T.J.) has been given to Parviz Khonsari, Shahanshah Aryamehr Ambassador, and the Permanent Iranian delegate at International Labour Office"
Kayhan, 16th August, 1976.

84. To give just a few examples of workers strikes before the 1953 Coup; on May 4, 1950, the workers of the textile factory of Shahi went on strike. March 19, 1951, 8,000 dockers of Ma'ashur. March 13, 1951, 40,000 oil workers of Abadan went on strike, it lasted twelve days. June 27, 1953, 20,000 brick workers went on strike, it lasted ten days.

uncover the historical facts about the Iranian Labour movement of yesterday and today and combine these with a theoretical debate. We choose this latter path. We are conscious that it is a very formidable task and requires the international co-operation of labour movements. We appeal to socialists throughout the world to make one important form of their expression of solidarity with the working class of Iran, and other countries, that they should find out who was the "cook" and "who paid the cost".

> .."The young Alexander conquered India.
> He alone?
> Caesar beat the Gauls.
> Without even a cook?...
>
> A victory on every page
> Who cooked the victory feast?
> A great man every ten years.
> Who paid the costs?
>
> So many reports
> So many questions." [85]

2. CIA

Let us turn now to the other arm of international capital, the American Central Intelligence Agency.

Even before the formation of SAVAK in 1957, the CIA had tried to infiltrate the Iranian Labour Movement immediately after the 1953 coup.

> "As early as 1953 plans were being made for a Ministry of Labour operated training centre for skilled workers." [86]

---

85. From "A worker's Questions While Reading" by Bertolt Brecht quoted in Village Life and Labour, edited by Raphael Samuel, Routledge & Kegan Paul, 1975.

86. Tehran Workers' Training Center, A Joint Effort of: Ministry of Labour, and the United States Operations Mission to Iran" undated document in British Museum, p.1. See picture next pages.

The construction of the training centre started early in 1957. The US Operations Mission contributed 10 million rials towards this and CENTO (the Middle East equivalent of NATO) provided five head instructors for the centre's operation.[87] The Centre was supposedly to be used to train skilled workers for Iranian industry but it was not long before such courses as "trade union studies" were introduced, and these were very similar to the courses which AIFLD (the American Institute for Free Labour Development) used to "train" 8,837 Chilean trade unionists - before the coup against Allende - in the "principles of democratic Trade Unionism" and in "small group infiltration techniques", "subversion of small groups", "the big lie tactic", "spotting the fraction", "terrorism and violence" and "what unions can do to promote democracy in Latin America."[88]

Later some of these Iranian trainees - in particular those who had shown most aptitude for assimilating the basic ideas - would be sent abroad to continue their studies in centres in Europe, Asia and the United States which were often funded and controlled either openly or secretly by the CIA or its front organisations such as AIFLD or ITS (International Trade Secretariats).

The Executive Board of Iranian Workers Organization like CNT (the Chilean fascist version of the TUC) is filled with workers who have gone through "training" for several years in Europe and North America in such institutions.[89]

---

87. Point IV US Aid Programme was used for this and similar work. More research needs to be done on exactly how much infiltration by the US had occurred even before the 1953 coup.

88. CIA and the Labour Movement, F. Hirsch & R. Fletcher, Spokesman Books, 1977, p. 35.

89. Evidence of such training courses comes out in all sorts of ways: Kayhan, August 11, 1976 reports an interview with five workers' "representatives" representing 5 million workers, one of whom was flourishing an English language edition of Kayhan and peppering his conversation with English (Continued P.71)

"H.E.A. Khosrovani and Eng. S. Sotoodeh award certificates."

" Completion Ceremony at the Workers Training (sic) at South Tehran
First Instructor Training Course - 42 Certificates awarded
L. to R. Ist row, Dr. Ganji, Minister of Roads; H.E. A. Khosrovani, Minister of Labor; Mr A. Read, U.K. Labor Attache; Mr. Harry Brenn, USOM Director; Mr F. Motamedi, Tech. Under Sect. MOL. "

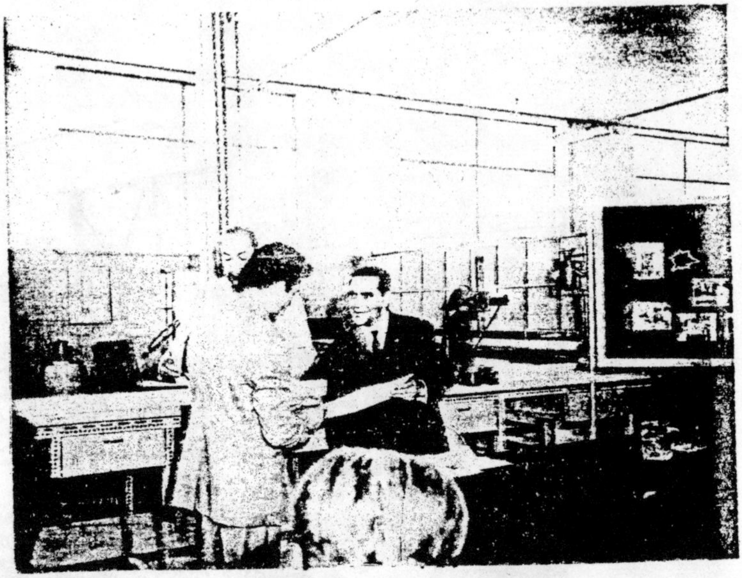

"The Minister of Labor H.E. A. Khosrovani and Eng. S. Sotoodeh present a certificate to a worker who completed the six month course at the Ministry's Training Center, South Tehran."

" A CENTO Instructor explains the work and test results of the trainees in the Welding Shop. The equipment of this and the other five shops was donated by the United States."

Let us compare the ideology of the American Institute of Free Labour Development and the Chilean Junta with that developed about the labour movement by the Iranian so-called workers' "leaders" and the we can see the CIA in the Iranian labour movement operation becoming more visible.

For instance:

Peter Grace, Chairman of the Board of AIFLD urges

> "co-operation between labour and management and an end to class struggle."[90]

Compare this with the following statement:

> "The Iranian revolution, they say (the theorists of the Iranian White Revolution-T.J.) has eradicated the concept of class (and by implication of class conflict) from the Iranian Society."[91]

and AIFLD

> "teaches workers to increase their company's business"[92]

Oscar Munoz after his return from the Front Royal Training Centre said:

> "The workers in general are participating in the reconstruction of the country."[93] (after the Chilean coup)

and

> "I (Prime Minister A. Hoveyda T.J.) am glad to observe that the workers themselves have brought up the idea of linking

---

89. cntd... words. We should ask, why was he doing this? And where had he learnt his English? Kayhan International edition is prepared for foreigners, and ordinary workers in Iran would be very unlikely to learn English unless they had been to school with the CIA.
90. P.17 of CIA and the Labour Movement, by F. Hirch and R. Fletcher, published by Spokesman Books, 1977.
91. Kayhan International, November 11, 1976.
92. CIA. Ibid. p.17.
93. Ibid. p.20.

wages and salaries to prductivity at their own Congress"(!)[94]

Harry Schauderman who had played some role in the subversive activities against Allende told the paid trainees:

> "Each nation in this Hemisphere must choose its own path, set its own priorities..."[95]

Compare this with Iranian regime views:

> "The document on the philosophy of the Iranian revolution is a strong defence of the uniqueness of the experience of each nation."[96]

The quotations which follow, whether they come from the Shah, members of his government or workers' "representatives", all express the same sentiments, often in very similar language. The basic ideas are: the unity of employers and workers, the necessity for hard work, and that class conflict has been ended and replaced, on the Shah's orders, by class harmony!

Mr Lotf'alah Rezakhahi, the "representative" of the workers of the weaving and spinning factories of Kashan, talked about:

> "the good relations which exist between employers and the workers in the weaving and spinning factories of Kashan."[97]

Mr Abdulah Ghorbanipour, the "representative" of the working people of the Engineering Co. of Karno said:

> "The workers of Iran do not feel lonely and alienated at their workplace because they participate in their work and therefore they should strive more and get better results."[98]

---

94. Kayhan International, November 10, 1976.
95. CIA. Ibid. p.36.
96. Kayhan International, November 11, 1976.
97. Etela'at, May 24, 1976.
98. Kayhan International, July 1, 1976.

Mr Mozafir Maro, the workers' "representative" of the Miral Factory which produces glass, said;

> "Now Iran is amongst the most progressive countries in the world."[99]

The workers' "representatives" constantly talk about how they were a 'dead force' or;

> "the workers were not taken into account before the Pahlevi Dynasty."[100]

Mr E. Khademi, workers' "representative" of a private stock company said:

> "You (workers) have progressed from nothingness to being."[101]

Then there was the worker in parliament in 1966 who said;

> "I am not a human being. I am a worker... His Imperial Majesty the Shahanshah for years knew about my loyalty and devotion and commanded that I be elected to the Majlis. Now I am proud to be the servant and soldier of His Majesty."[102]

Then the workers' "representative", Mr Bakshi of the Glass Co. of Ghazvin:

> "Greetings to the very meritous leader, Shahanshah Araymehr, from the Nation of Iran and particularly from the Iranian workers for lifting up the chains of slavery and bondage from the necks of the Iranian workers and setting them free."[103]

---

99. Iran Radio, October 14, 1976.
100. Kayhan International, October 12, 1976.
101. Kayhan International, August 15, 1976.
102. The Politics of Iran, by James Alban Bill, published by Charles E. Merrill Pub. Company, Colombus, Ohio, 1972.
103. Kayhan International, October 9, 1976.

The General Secretary of the Syndicates of the workers of the BIG Lorry Repair Workshop of Tehran, Mr Reza Noori-Zadeh, talks of the:

"Shahanshah who built a free and prosperous Iran."[104]

(Our emphasis)

Those who are familiar with the lack of any forms of freedom, except Freedom for International Capital, must realise there are so-called workers' representatives who use "freedom" in exactly the same way as the CIA, or AIFLD, uses it.

Mr Abkari, the President of the Iranian Workers Organisation explains very vividly, the meaning of this usage of "freedom" and "democracy" when he says;

> "Today the situation in our country from the point of view of social security, political and economic stability is in such a good way that the advanced countries of the world can invest in our country without any worries and problems. One of the best examples of this foreign investment is this huge unit of Bayer-Iran Shimi and Bayer Farma of Iran."[105]

In conclusion, Iranian opposition groups have paid little attention to concrete studies about the nature of CIA operations in the Iranian labour movement whereas they are aware of the U.S. Military operations in Iran. It is reported that since 1950, the Military Assistance Programme has trained 320,000[106] whereas AIFLD has trained 243,668 during the same period. But these 243,668 are only for Latin America and the Caribbean area. But if we add the figure of people trained by AIFLD to infiltrate Asia and Africa then we realise that the extent and scope of the labour movement infiltration by the CIA is even larger than that of MAP. Iran can be no exception to this rule, i.e. the scale and scope of CIA infiltration in the Iranian labour movement must be very high, but this area has been neglected by most Iranian opposition groups and we should not forget this.

---

104. Iran Radio, October 11, 1976.

105. Iran Radio, November 3, 1976.

106. CIA. Ibid. p.11.

STRIKES

1. Conditions of Work:

Before we consider strikes and other forms of protest by the workers in Iran, we must say something about the life of the workers at work and the actual conditions under which they carry out their jobs.

There are many things which are of concern to the workers besides their wages: job security, redundancy, who makes the decisions about work methods, work discipline, manning levels, a say in management decisions, etc. In Iran all these matters are dealt with by management - there is no trace of industrial democracy.[107]

In capitalist countries like Britain much has been done to improve the physical conditions under which labour is performed. Safety and health standards are laid down and workers in Britain play some important role in ensuring that they are carried out stringently.

But in Iran the picture is very different. In most workplaces and factories there is:

- no identification of health hazards like fumes, or noxious chemicals or other materials used in various processes, and no protection against damage to the workers' health (through lung or skin diseases, for instance);

- no proper lighting, heating, cleaning or air-conditioning of the workplace;

- no proper provision of lockers, space for changing clothes, hot and cold running water, showers, lavatories, soap, towels;

- no first-aid equipment, industrial nurses, medical inspections;

- no limits on carrying heavy weights and a lack of mechanical aids for this;
- no proper guards for machinery;

---

107. It is obvious to all that "industrial democracy" is different from "workers democracy", the latter of which can only be achieved in a socialist society.

- no protective clothing such as overalls, reinforced footwear, goggles, gloves, leather spats and sleeves, ear muffs;

- no surveys of noise levels - with the result that many workers go deaf;

- no fire precautions or drills or provision for storage of flammable materials - almost every day the censored Iranian press are allowed to report fires in some workplaces; perhaps the government thinks of this as a "natural calamity"?

The net effect of all these unsafe working conditions is that every day a few workers are killed and thousands are injured.[108]

So it can be seen that the situation in Iran is at least as bad as that which arose in Britain at the beginning of the Industrial Revolution.

In such a situation the individual workers experience a very great degree of alienation in their own working lives. This is not a matter of concern to the authorities who have a pool of unemployed or under-employed workers to call on. But the workers who are conscious of their "unfree activity", who are aware that it is;

> "...performed in the service, under the dominion, the coercion, and the yoke of another man"[109]

and who understand their condition and that of their brothers and sisters; who see themselves and them treated like soldiers in barracks without any freedom to express their grievances and get them redressed; and who see their country spend over £8 billion on armaments while their working conditions remain so apalling - also feel the great necessity for their fellow workers to unite and fight for change.

---

108. According, TUC, "Health & Safety at work", January, 1977, "On an average working day in this country four workers will die, and over 3,000 will be injured seriously enough to lose three or more days from work. The total number of injured runs into millions every year." - p.5.

For a country like Iran, you can imagine how many workers are killed and injured daily.

109. Karl Marx, "Economic and Philosophic Manuscripts of 1844" in Marx, cntd...

2. Socio-economic Causes of Strikes:

Earlier we quoted the Financial Times to show that the Shah's claim that:

"...there is not one minute's strike"

in Iran to be absolutely false; but we should add here emphatically that no western reporter for the capitalist press can get a true picture of the magnitude of the strikes in Iran. We quote the Financial Times, Le Monde, or any other western source, not because they are our only source of information, but because their authority is recognised in this country.

Lord Thorneycroft took a more realistic view of the situation than the Shah's blinkered one: strikes are a common aspect of all highly developed economies. The Iranian workers, far from not striking, are stepping up their fight for better wages and conditions - both physical and work relations. There will be more and more strikes in Iran for the following main reasons:

1. The number of industrial workers is rising very rapidly - from the ILO figure of 773,000 in 1956 (11 per cent of the labour force) to an estimated 2,100,000 in March 1977 (20 per cent).

2. The number of modern mechanical workshops which employ more than 10 workers is rising but the number of huge industrial complexes which employ thousands of workers is still very small.

3. The industrial workforce which has recently left the countryside is increasingly breaking away from the countryside mentality which sees production problems as being solvable on an individual basis (if the peasant works his own land, for instance). In the factories a more collective approach to their daily problems has to be taken, and so they organise in their factories.

4. The propaganda put out by the regime, and particularly on Iran Radio's daily half-hour programmes for workers, is not having the effects desired by the authorities. (The workers are told that they must work hard, be disciplined, respect

---

109. cntd... and Engels, Collected Works, Volume 3, p.279. Lawrence and Wishart, 1975.

the authorities; there is no basic conflict between worker and employer and any minor difficulty which arises can easily be sorted out by the Ministry of Labour which cares for the workers' rights and interests; wages and working and living conditions have improved enormously due to their kind benefactor, the Shah, who has given them everything they possess; anyone who does not agree and conform to all this will be dealt with severely).

5. The Shah's new decree that every patriotic worker should become politically active in his party, Rastakhiz, (and only in his - all others are banned) is having two contradictory effects. On the one hand, a tiny minority who are after high salaries and privileges and who have received AIFLD "training", are littering the rostrums and conference halls at meetings organised by the Rastakhiz Party. On the other hand, the large majority of the workers who are dragged to these political meetings, and filled with government propaganda, may not at first find it easy to resist such glowing promises as are made, but their daily experiences more and more contradict the official picture presented to them, and they are looking for answers elsewhere.

6. Various opposition groups which were either mainly discussion groups or were engaged in other forms of struggle are beginning to establish direct contact with the workers.

7. The prices of basic foods and necessities of life are increasing and there is an acute shortage of basic foods such as meat, milk, etc.; and the cost of accomodation and the extreme shortage of housing, are two of the greatest difficulties facing workers in big cities such as Tehran and Tabriz, etc. [109a]

8. The economic crisis, which has been created by the following major factors, is having a great effect:

a) the effect of the recession in international capitalism which is affecting the Iranian economy which is heavily linked with it, causing for example, a higher proportion of the Iranian GNP to be spent on imports - $15 billion annually;
b) the two-tier price of oil system in OPEC which slashed Iranian revenues by billions of pounds - over £2 billion.

109a. According to the Guardian, April 19, 1977, the official Iranian rate of inflation is 15.5 per cent; our own conservative estimate is that it is between 20 and 25%.

c) phenomenal spending on sophisticated armaments which will soon reach $20 billion;

d) the total failure of the agricultural policy and the extreme shortage of agricultural products, leading to imports of foodstuffs previously plentifully produced in Iran; one German estimate (Handelsblatt, 10.8.76) is a cost of 4 bn DM annually.

e) the widespread corruption amongst government officials who squander alot of money; even some western reporters who might have been misled into believing that such a regime could eliminate corruption have had to report that:

"...corruption has been far from eliminated";[110]

f) spending huge amounts of money on "prestige projects" which are not viable even according to capitalist standards.

The net effect of all this has been increasing unemployment, and even a reduction in the basic wages in some areas (see strike reported below at Tabriz) although excessive overtime can still be worked.

The most direct response to this crisis by workers has been strikes. The cause of strikes is the capitalist mode of production, and this mode of production has many-sided repressive effects on the workers - economic, political, psychological, etc. But most strikes present particular demands which, on the face of it, may be only economic.

The demands have usually been economic, but particularly in the context of Iran we must understand that all 'economic' demands are also 'political' because they bring workers into direct confrontation with the state. This means challenging the authority of the despotic regime of the Shah. Not many strikes in Britain neccessarily lead to a 'trial of strength' with the state but in Iran every striker must decide whether he can face the combined might of SAVAK, police and army, with the consequence of being wounded, killed, imprisoned or tortured, or at least losing his job or being demoted, and in this sense, every strike in Iran is a 'genuine trial of strength'.

---

110. Financial Times, December 13, 1976. An effect of all this and other factors is a budget deficit of between $2.5 and $4 billion which has caused the slashing of social services plans and consequent hardships for all workers.

THE LABOUR LAW IN IRAN IS ABSOLUTELY SILENT ABOUT UNEMPLOYMENT BENEFITS

This picture shows unemployed workers (including skilled painters) standing at the corner of Lalezar and Manucheri Streets in Tehran.

They are waiting in the hope that some employer will want them.

At the same time in Tehran and other big cities there are many slums - and people without proper homes - but the government which can find the money to put up useless memorials to the monarchy (like the Shahyad Monument) does not finance a housebuilding programme for the workers, in spite of billions of pounds of oil revenue.

The Guardian, April 19, 1977, reports that the Prime Minister has provided "an example by slashing his staff by 20 per cent. The Health Minister followed by also slashing 1,400 jobs. The Interior Ministry axed even more - 1,700."

Every striker in Iran challenges explicitly the present social rights "given" to the working class. Strikers challenge the ideology of the regime which recognises only "economic" rights in industrial conflict.

As we have already seen, a conciliation process has been officially set up and according to Iran Radio the following principles are the governing factors:

1. "...the factory must operate in order that the worker benefit from it;"
2. "...the worker must be satisfied and be able to provide for his expenses in order to work with interest and strength;"
3. "...every factory or industrial institution is a part of the whole national economy of the country and the state cannot remain indifferent to its fate".[111]

The regime does not allow the worker to use the strike as a weapon to defend his interests. Even the ILO to which Iran is a member state has at least recognised this in theory:

> "The Committee on Freedom of Association set up by the Governing Body of the ILO has laid down and acted upon the principle that "the right to strike is generally admitted as an integral part of the general right of workers and their organisations to defend their economic interests" (Jenks, The International protection of trade union freedom, 1957, p.370); and its existence or absence may therefore be used as indicative of the compliance or non-complance(sic) by a member state with the standards laid down in the freedom of associations conventions."[112]

---

111. Iran Radio, July 27, 1976.
112. Otto Kahn-Freund & Bob Hepple - "Laws against strikes" published by the Fabian Society, Research Series 305, p.16.
Why is the ILO silent about the way the Iranian regime violates workers' rights? Shouldn't Amnesty International enquire into the nature of such a silence?

Under these conditions of suppression of every form of political liberty, various forms of struggle merge with each other.[113]

And as Marx says:

> "...every movement in which the working class comes out as a class against the ruling classes and tries to coerce them by pressure from without is a political movement..."[114]

In this sense, every strike in Iran, although its demands may be economic, is a "political movement" because it is also a struggle for the rights of the whole working class - the right to strike.

Strikers in Iran suffer very greatly and it is difficult to measure this. In Britain very occasionally in the last century, striking and demonstrating workers have been shot; the Tolpuddle Martyrs were transported; and many thousands of workers have lost their jobs because they fought for their rights. But in Iran the degree of suffering is much worse - every striker faces the possibility of death. Another differing factor is that the public are prevented from giving any forms of open support to strikers. Although in both countries most strikes may be unofficial and some unconstitutional, those in Iran are treated in practice as "crimes" and are suppressed accordingly.

3. News of Strikes

Here is an incomplete and fragmentary list of strikes for the period February 1976 to July 1976, the period for whichwe have been able to check the authenticity of the reports.

In February, the workers at Shahbaf factory (textiles) of Rashat demanded higher wages. The strike lasted only a few hours but in spite of the police and SAVAK agents threat, the employers accepted the demands of the workers. One report

---

113. V.I. Lenin "What is to be done?" Selected Works, Volume 1, p.208, Progress Publishers, Moscow, 1970.
114. Marx, Engels, Lenin, "Anarchism and Anarcho-Syndicalism, p.57, published by Progress Publishers, Moscow, 1972.

also indicates that the workers broke some machinery.

In April, about 3,000 agricultural workers of Pars Abad in Maghan plain, who work a 12-hour day and whose women workers are paid half the wages of the men, staged a strike. Their demand was the implementation of the "Labour Law" and especially the 8-hour day and equal wages for women. The armed police attacked the workers and broke up the strike.

In May, the moulders in the furnaces of Marand, Tabriz and Ardabil, staged a strike because their piece-rate wages for 1,000 bricks had been reduced by 12 per cent. The grievance was eventually sent to arbitration and we do not know the result yet.

In the same month, the Sangrood miners of the coal mine near Shahrud, started a strike. The workers, in order not to be identified by SAVAK agents, blackened their faces. The employers were frightened and locked themselves in the cupboards and armed forces surrounded the 4,000 miners. The workers' demands were for an increase in wages proportional to the increase in the cost of living and for safety measures at work. No threat changed the determination of the miners and they resisted every single threat. The government and the employers joined together for consultation and they were forced to accept the miners' demands. The strike ended successfully but one report indicated that after the strike about 50-70 workers were sent to Semen and Daghan prisons for torture so that it could be found out who were the "ring-leaders" since during the strike SAVAK agents could not spot these "ring-leaders".

Also in May, about 10,000 workers in the brick furnaces of Tabriz and Ardabil, staged a strike. The strike lasted one week and the workers succeeded in gaining their demands for 50 per cent higher wages.

May Day - 3,000 workers of the chintz textile factory of Tehran, staged a strike for higher wages. The whole factory was surrounded by armed soldiers. One report indicates that there was a clash between the workers and the soldiers and dozens of workers were killed. Amongst those workers who were killed was someone named Changizi. The strike lasted 15 days. Immediately two other textile factories of the Atlas Group, and other factories located at Razmara Street, staged a strike.

In May, the workers of the Packing Factory of Iran, which is part of the Behshahr Industrial Group, started a one-day strike for a wage increase. In this strike many leaflets which were prepared clandestinely, were distributed. The demands of these workers were not met and they staged another strike on August 30, 1976, (Monday). On Tuesday the strike spread throughout the whole factory. In the afternoon the workers of other sections joined them. The next day all workers of the sections joined the strike and it spread throughout the whole of BIG. The so-called workers' representative stood shoulder to shoulder with the employers who were begging the workers to go back to work. But the workers ignored his pleas and even refused to listen to him. Eventually the employers asked for a 20-day period to consider the demands of the workers. The workers agreed to this and went back to work on a go-slow basis. The demands of the workers were:

1. A 35 per cent increase in wages;
2. The payment of housing benefits at the current rate of prices;
3. A definite 3 hours overtime daily.

The following leaflet was written, printed and distributed clandestinely in other factories by the BIG workers:

> "A Way Out For The Workers Is - Unity And Organisation"
>
> "We, workers of the Behshar Industrial Group have gone on strike once more because the authorities have not paid attention to our demands which are rooted in the unbearable and difficult conditions of life during this dark period."
>
> "Under such present conditions, when an anti-people's regime rules, we are even deprived of the most basic trade union rights. The Ministry of Labour and its phoney representatives are no more than puppets in the hands of the capitalist thieves."

"Only through uniting ourselves, isolating the spies of the employers, and a united strike can we achieve our demands. We can stand against plunderers such as Lajvardi, Sabet Pasal', Reza'eis, etc., who are all arms-folded-on-the-chest servants of foreign capital."

"Therefore comrades strive to create a united organisation for more longlasting strikes which at this stage of the struggle is the only weapon of use to the workers and toilers."

"Greetings to our militant comrades in other factories."

"Hold dear the memory of those martyrs who sacrificed their lives for the emancipation of the working class."

"Long live the unity and solidarity of the toiling peoples of Iran."

"May the rule of thieves and plunderers be destroyed. (Our solidarity guarantees our Victory)."

In June, the workers at a cement factory in Isfahan, started a strike for higher wages. The strike ended after four days and the workers' demands were met.

Also in June, the workers of the spinning mill of Simin in Isfahan, the 7,000 textile factory workers of Shahnaz and 1,400 woollen textile workers, started a strike for higher wages. The strike spread very fast through Isfahan city - known as the Manchester of Iran - and the Ministry of Labour was frightened of a general strike in Isfahan, so they met some of the workers' demands and the strike ended.

The workers at Aladin, which employs less than 200 workers, started a strike for higher wages. There is no further news about the outcome of this strike except that a few workers were taken to SAVAK headquarters for interrogation.

In June again, the workers of the Minou Food Industries, struck for higher wages.

In July, the workers of Behshahr Industrial Group (BIG) turner section, staged a strike for higher wages. The strike lasted about 4 days and the workers' demands were met.

The Iranian mass media implicitly - probably in their ignorance of the various forms of industrial conflicts - are admitting the existence of protests.

According to C. Kerr:

> "The strike is the most common and most visible expression. But conflict with the employer may also take the form of peaceful bargaining and grievance handling, of boycotts, of political action, restriction of output, of sabotage, of absenteeism, or of personnel turnover. Several of these forms, such as sabotage, restriction of output, absenteeism, and turnover, may take place on an individual as well as an organised basis and constitute alternatives to collective action. Even the strike is of many varieties."[115]

At the present time the Iranian mass media, are complaining about workers 'lack of discipline', 'absenteeism','personnel turnover', and in order to solve this problem they have introduced more repressivè labour law regulations.

And they confess:

> "We have to admit with sorrow that the spirit of working hard, and increasing productivity has decreased in our country in recent years... and one of the most important factors which causes this situation is the same secret, shrewd, propaganda of the subversive enemies of Iran."[116]

We can take this confession in two ways:

If what the spokesman of the regime says is true, it proves one thing, that SAVAK

---

115. C. Kerr, Labour and Management in Industrial Society, p.171, New York, 1964.

116. Tehran Economist, January 29, 1977.

and CIA, in spite of all their "efficiency", are defeated at the hands of the "subversive enemy", (i.e. propagandists for basic workers' rights) and they have managed to 'infiltrate' the labour movement and 'agitate' among the workers.

We do ask the regime this question:

If the workers are contented and satisfied and "have progressed from nothingness to being", how is it that these "tiny insignificant subversive enemies" can turn this upside down?

To accept such a conclusion, we should either admit that these "tiny insignificant subversive enemies" are after all, strong, significant and powerful, or the workers are "stupid" and behave like sheep!

All this unrest, both strikes and other forms of protest, is mainly a 'spontaneous' response to the actual conditions and relations of life and work which we have set out in this work; and to the fact that despite all the Shah's repressive techniques, more activists are coming into the labour movement and are recognising the vanguard position of the workers.

4. Why No Report of Strikes?

Why is our list of strikes incomplete?

The Shah in his numerous interviews has explicitly admitted:

a) that there are political prisoners - but of course only 1/25th of the highest number estimated by Amnesty International; he admits to 3-4,000[117], and

b) that torture is used - of course never admitting the truly brutal nature of the torture.[118]

---

117. One of the Shah's leading henchmen, Parviz Sabeti, deputy director of SAVAK admitted in September, 1976, that there were 3,200 political prisoners. A.I. quoting Washington Post, September 3, 1976.

118. In reply to a question about torture from Lord Chalfont in an interview quoted in, The Shah, by Margaret Laing, (Sidgwick & Jackson, 1977) p.214, the Shah

cntd...

But, as we have seen, the Shah does not admit that the workers ever go on strike, even for one minute.

The same mass media which spread distorted ideas about the cause and effect of strikes in this country, are behind the conspiracy of silence about strikes in Iran. For example, those who financed and wrote the following statement about British Leyland toolmakers' strike in February 1977, were on the one hand silent about strikes in Iran and on the other hand, glorified the Shah's regime.

> "It is a fact [that the strike is against the interests of the workers] so simple and obvious that even a child could understand. Why then cannot the Leyland workers themselves see it?"[119]

The strikers are;

> "...motivated by selfishness, nothing more..."[120]

> "What they cannot see is that every strike is a nail in their own coffin. Every time a dispute halts production of Leyland cars customers go elsewhere, perhaps never to return. It is as simple as that."[121]

More specifically, why is the Shah silent?

Because if he confesses to this, then how can his apologists such as Ms Laing, justify the existence of his regime?

---

118. cntd...said;

"...I should say anything goes..."

(Ms Laing, in an interview in The Guardian of February 24, 1977, admitted that the Shah lived as a despot, refused his people basic freedoms, violated human rights on a massive scale where people did not agree with his ideas; she went on to justify all this by saying that Iran was "backward". We wonder just how much Ms Laing really knows about Iran, its history and its people.)

119. 120. 121. Coventry Evening Telegraph, February 18, 1977. Compare this with the same paper's article about the "Industrial Relations" in Iran National Factory - Chrysler.

The Shah is extremely conscious that the real danger which threatens his peacock throne comes from the workers, and that is the reason why he, with the help of CIA "theoreticians", has designed numerous schemes to deceive the workers.

The regime, being conscious of the danger of spreading news of the workers' fight does the following things:

1. Does not permit the mass media to report any news of the workers' strikes (we know of such strikes, as reported above, and for one year we have thoroughly read 99.9 per cent of the copies of Kayhan, the semi-official newspaper, and not one report of any strike by workers appeared).

2. Those who attempt to spread such news inside or outside Iran are treated mercilessly by SAVAK.

3. Foreign reporters in Iran are not allowed to report any news of strikes. To give an example, it is interesting to note that the Financial Times reporter, who wrote about many subjects in Iran from June 28, 1975, to July 21, 1976, did not report any details of one single strike, yet suddenly on July 21, 1976, the Financial Times says that strikes are increasing in Iran.

The effects of these methods are:

1. Various groups which have contacts with Iran approach the mass media in western countries and give them the news about the workers' strikes. They usually refuse to publish this news on the grounds that the source of the news is not reliable and the mass media cannot independently verify the truth-value of it. Even some of the organisations which in this country are concerned about the rights of workers, have fallen into this trap and refuse to publish such news unless it is given to them by someone who shares their own brand of political ideology.

2. News of the workers' fight comes from various groups active within Iran and no group has an all-over network throughout the factories and workshops in Iran. Even the combined forces of all groups put together don't have an all-over network throughout the factories and workshops. This means each group will have a certain limited account from certain factories but because of political differences amongst

various groups they are suspicious of each other's news. In Britain, even if attitudes to struggles differ, the actual struggles themselves are at least reported.[122]

5. Why Strikes Deserve More Publicity

The scarcity of news about Iranian labour movement, which is caused by the present regime, has prevented the workers and activists in the British labour movement knowing the real picture.

Occasionally a western newspaper tries to make some sort of investigation into conditions in Iran[123] but these are few and far between - and there is a great need for investigative journalists to probe beneath the surface of the Shah's regime and discover the facts about the Iranian workers' conditions and their struggles.

In order to understand how important it is to give the maximum publicity and support to these strikes we must have a much more detailed conception of the conditions under which they happen.

The presence of SAVAK in every factory (where, for example, they check the records of the employees before they are employed to make sure that 'undesirable' persons do not get work there) makes it very difficult, almost impossible, to establish non-clandestine contact between workers for the purpose of independent organisation which is not approved by the regime. SAVAK aims to bring under

---

122. But we believe under the present conditions in Iran, one might recognise how important and vital it is to get hold of news of workers' struggles and how the Shah tries to cover them up. Under these conditions a refusal to publicise such news on the grounds that it has been put out by a group whose political beliefs are different from ours, will contribute to strengthening the Shah's regime. This point may help us to understand the extent of the damage the various sectarian groups may be causing to the Iranian labour movement.

123. See Le Monde Diplomatique, May, 1975, and the Financial Times which was already quoted.

complete surveillance every movement of the workers; but here we must draw a very clear distinction between what SAVAK aims at and what actually in practice it can achieve. Unfortunately some opposition groups have confused SAVAK's own propaganda and what actually happens in practice and have come to believe that SAVAK has been successful in bringing all factories under complete surveillance.[124] They think thus because they are confusing SAVAK's methods and their effects. It is true that SAVAK is ruthless and its brutality cannot be exaggerated; but what can be exaggerated is the effect of this brutality and ruthlessness, so that opponents feel helpless before it.[125]

---

124. Le Monde, October 5, 1976, writes:

"Fear of SAVAK it is said in Tehran, is the beginning of wisdom..."

Fear of SAVAK for the workers means the beginning of their total defeat. That is the reason why the workers who start struggles against the regime, are not afraid of SAVAK, but are conscious of its brutality and dirty tricks and they carry out their activities cautiously. This consciousness makes them invent various ingenious ways to minimize SAVAK infiltration into their own clandestine activities. A successful strike vindicates that SAVAK agents can be ineffective. We should never forget that one of the main activities of SAVAK is to spread fear amongst the population about its strength and almightiness.

125. The CBS TV film already mentioned has now been shown in New York in their "Sixty Minute Programme". It reveals the story of a journalist who was given the task of assassinating some of the Shah's opponents. According to the same film SAVAK has despatched an assassination squad to western Europe and North America to kill those Iranians who are active campaigners against the Shah's regime. There also are indications that there is close co-operation between SAVAK and their counterparts in various countries. It is true that under these conditions the activities of CRTURI and other organisations in this country - and in other countries - will be watched closely by SAVAK. Vigilance on the part of the labour movement is always required in order to protect activists from the unwelcome attention of home, and overseas, police interest. Nonetheless, to propagate the myth of SAVAK's deadly efficiency is to play into its hands.

The mere start of a strike means a declaration of war against the combined forces of employers, government, the police, the armed forces of SAVAK and even some workers' "representatives", not to mention here the important problem of "blacklegs" exacerbated by the high level of unemployment. Employers wanting to use such scab labour are given every help by the government, for instance, use of transport to bring such people from one city to another. It has been reported that military planes have been used to bring in Pakistani blackleg labour to help break a strike.

The start of a strike shatters the notion that SAVAK is all-powerful. It means the workers have managed somehow, in spite of the presence of SAVAK agents, to communicate with one another, to exchange experiences and grievances, and come to certain conclusions; war has to be declared. This means that the workers have learned how to fight against the secret police and have developed a very complex network of underground communication systems.[126] The declaration of war under these conditions confirms a certain degree of organisation. The employer contacts the workers' "representative", most of whom are against the workers, and the Ministry of Labour. They start "peaceful" negotiations with the workers. As the workers resist, verbal threats are first uttered, then put into practice. The factory is surrounded by armed forces of soldiers and police. This kind of action destroys the regime's propaganda that the government is caring and defends the workers' interests and rights. Two armies face each other, one unarmed and one armed. One side asks for the most elementary rights, such as a decent wage so that all can afford to maintain themselves. The other refuses to negotiate. The Commander-in-Chief of the armed forces, the Shah, is informed of the war which has broken out. Consultations are held at all levels to try to find a quick way out of this "unacknowledgeable" problem. Usually they come up with a combined offer of partial concessions to the workers' demands and some use of terror against a few workers (i.e. they arrest or even shoot them) hoping by this example to demoralise the rest into giving in quickly.

---

126. Just analysing this in great detail reveals a good deal about the level of political consciousness of the workers. It must be added that the prerequisite of a successful underground struggle is the relatively high level of working-class political consciousness.

When a strike is successful - for example, as happened last year in the Shahrud miners' strike - the combined forces of the army, SAVAK, the employers and even sometimes the so-called workers' representatives, are forced to accept their defeat at the hands of the unarmed army. A successful strike will have a destructive effect on the daily propaganda forced into the workers' minds, i.e. that 99.9 per cent of the population enjoy secure living and working conditions; and because of this, that 99.9 per cent support the regime wholeheartedly. The regime also has well-armed forces. All this makes the regime invincible - and Iran is a "heaven". All this special progress and these achievements were possible only because of the great leadership of the Shah. The argument continues; because 99.9 per cent of the population are well-off and support the present regime, then the extremely small minority who are against it are either misled by imported ideologies which are alien to the concrete conditions of Iran ; or they are the paid agents of "black" or red "imperialists"; or they suffer from psychological complexes[127]; or, last but most dangerously, they are really SAVAK agents who have set up these organisations to find out what and who are against the regime.

---

127. Radio Iran, August 14, 1976.

"Dear Worker Friends,

"Remember that whenever you are criticised it is because you have accomplished an important task and consequently have attracted the attention of the public. Or, as the proverb says, "Nobody beats a dead person". A person who is more important and more popular, his personality and ideas will be the target of poisonous arrows. Who are these people who throw these poisonous arrows? They are people who have inferiority complexes and who are debased. These neurotic people enjoy attacking the important, great and constructive people. These neurotic people think that by attacking and criticising these great persons they gain a feeling of greatness. They have to pour water on the fire of their own jealousy and revengfulness through their attacks and criticisms. They get relief by doing this. You should consider their criticisms as praise and regard them as nonsensical."

(Our emphases)

These people become "subversives" or "terrorists". Since this small number of people should not be allowed to endanger the happiness of the 99.9 per cent they will be dealt with ruthlessly - and their strength is absolutely peripheral to life in Iran.

So runs the official version!

A successful strike explodes these empty phrases, exposing them for the lies they are.

The workers are not satisfied with their conditions and they are not happy with the government's policies and they do not expect peaceful negotiations to give them their rights; they have to fight for their rights. They do not need to be thankful for the things which they are promised, or "given" by the Shah. Above all, they destroy the myths put forward by SAVAK that the regime's strength and power is absolute and that those who oppose this regime will be smashed.

A successful strike reveals the potential of the untapped strength of the workers. It shows that when workers are determined, united and organised, they can bring one of the most brutal states to its knees and make it unwillingly accept their demands. The effect of a successful strike on other factories is enormous.

Almost every single worker can identify himself or herself with strikers, because strikers are "average" workers; whereas it is not so likely that every worker could identify himself or herself with individual heroes acting on their behalf.

The strikes, occupations and other actions make the workers realise more and more that the act of emancipation requires independent action by themselves; and above all, that they do not need all those "philanthropists" who want to "do something for the workers". These latter, can be confident that the workers, provided they are organised, act in unity, and have a correct strategy, will not need any "alms" from generous "do-gooders". Even those strikes which are not successful will teach workers how to improve their methods of organisation and how to intensify the war in the next battle.

Under these unfavourable conditions - the difficulties of spreading news of workers' strikes, protests, etc. - and yet the importance of doing so - one finds most Iranian opposition groups outside Iran spend almost all their time and activity on political prisoners, although almost all of them pay lip service to the idea that every form of struggle against the regime should be given maximum publicity and assistance. These groups have not yet undertaken a systematic theoretical analysis of why they concern themselves in practice almost solely with political prisoners.

Why is there so much of a gap between theory and practice when it comes to giving publicity and assistance to the workers' conditions and struggles?

Those who in practice are mainly concerned with defending political prisoners forget that these political prisoners can only be defended effectively if the following points are remembered:

1. The working and living conditions of the millions in the society to which the political prisoners belong should be portrayed in a very systematic and detailed manner.

2. Outside Iran effective material and moral assistance for the defence of political prisoners can only be given by the labour movements.

3. Even those reactionary people who support the Shah because they see him as the only force able to bring about changes in Iran must be shown that this is not the case; their arguments and beliefs must be countered, even though they themselves may find this difficult to accept.

4. To be a political prisoner is in one sense a defeat, since the prisoner has been caught; but in the wider sense it is a victory because such prisoners bear witness to the struggles of the many and carry on the fight even in gaols. But a balance must be struck between consideration for their welfare and emphasis on the continuing battles of those millions of workers making up the labour movement in Iran who daily experience the full rigours of the Shah's so-called "benevolent" regime of inflation, harsh discipline at work, low wages, bad housing at exorbitant prices and poor medical care (life expectancy of the workers in Iran, for instance, being officially 45 years, but we believe in practice, much less).

5. It is not enough to demand the release of political prisoners without asking who can release them, and how do we mobilise support for this?

What we are advocating is simply that more support should be given to the struggles of the workers and the defence of the workers - political - prisoners, rather than the intellectual political prisoners. Those who doubt the validity of such a proposition should write a counter-proposal and those who consider it correct should put it into practice.

INTERNATIONAL SOLIDARITY - 1. AMNESTY INTERNATIONAL

As late as May 14, 1976[128], Amnesty International had not 'adopted' any workers as prisoners of conscience in Iran and those who were 'adopted' tended to be "students and intellectuals".

Information about prisoners in Iran is never easy to obtain because of the very strict censorship exercised by the Shah's government. That information which has come out has tended to come from students and professional people[129] and their knowledge, whether as friends and colleagues, or as fellow-prisoners, is inclined to be solely of their own kind. Workers, some of whom may be illiterate, do not end up in the same cells as professors.

Before November 1976 AI had not issued any statements on imprisoned trade unionists in Iran. Press statements, annual reports, the 1972 Trial Procedures for Political Prisoners and the 1973 AI International Report on Torture all have highlighted Iran's terrible record on the violation of human rights, on torture, on imprisonment for political reasons and on unexplainable deaths. The AI November 1976 Briefing on Iran marks a great step forward in respect of recognising that trade unionists and workers are taking part in the struggle against despotism in Iran. On our estimate, trade unionists and workers form a sizeable percentage of the political prisoners in that country.

---

128. David Simpson, Director, British Section, AI, in a letter to CRTURI.

129. See article on "Terror in Iran" by Reza Baraheni in the New York Review,

cntd...

Iran
Systematische Folterungen!
78 Hinrichtungen in 6 Monaten!
ai
amnesty international

We hope that the statement, Section 10 of the Briefing, which we here reprint with AI's permission, will be the first of many on those trade unionists and workers who are suffering so severely in their fight for democracy and free trade unions in Iran.

"In addition to the violations already referred to there is little respect demonstrated for human rights in many other areas of Iranian life. Freedom of speech and association are non-existent. The press is strictly censored and has been dramatically curtailed in recent years since the Shah decreed that every newspaper with a circulation of less than 3,000 and periodicals with a circulation of less than 5,000 should be shut down. Trade unions are illegal and workers' protests are dealt with severely, sometimes resulting in imprisonment and deaths. Political activity is restricted to participation in the Rastakhiz Party. Some Iranians have difficulty in obtaining, or are refused, passports. This restriction on freedom of movement applies especially to released political prisoners and members of their families. Academic freedom is also restricted and students and teachers are kept under surveillance by SAVAK..."

Mr D. Simpson, Director of the British Section of Amnesty International says:

"Our government supplies vast quantities of military supplies to Iran. UK firms compete for business from Iran. British

---

129. cntd... October 28, 1976:

"Imagine 100,000 educated men and women in prison while 75 per cent of the whole nation is illiterate! Imagine hundreds of doctors in prison when every fifty villages in the country have only one doctor! Imagine roads awaiting construction while engineers are rotting in jails! "

> scientists, medical and university personnel apply for jobs there. We must ensure that if arms are sold, if business is done, if jobs are applied for, it must be with a full understanding of the fear in which ordinary Iranians live. Anyone who has known Iranians in this country, let alone in Iran, will know of their reluctance to speak about the torture and imprisonment of their compatriots, for the fear that they may be spied upon by SAVAK agents. As a major ally of the Iranian regime, Britain has a special position from which to demand an end to repression in Iran."[130]

In passing, we must note that even this excellent statement of the potential power of Britain against the Shah, reveals at the same time, the belief in the omnipotence of SAVAK.

Every single refusal on the part of Iranians to reveal their identity[131] and discuss their political views openly has been incorrectly interpreted as being due to fear of SAVAK. This false interpretation has been widely disseminated by most western journalists and some Iranian amateur activists throughout the world. One of the causes of such misunderstanding is the inability to comprehend the complex rule of underground activity. It must be remembered that there are very many Iranians who will not give their real names to anyone because they are observing the rules of underground activity.

2. TUC

As late as May, 1976, the TUC had no official policy or even knowledge of the apalling conditions of the workers and the lack of independent and democratic trade unions in Iran.

---

130. "The Way", AEU, February, 1977.

131. Many Iranian militants sign their writings with pseudonyms.

"The International Confederation of Free Trade Unions are closely following labour and trade union developments in Iran, but we are not aware that they have issued any statement."[132]

As the campaign, through its publications, speakers, personal contacts with trade unionists, spread the news and knowledge about conditions in Iran, the British labour movement responded promptly although still on a very small scale. Trade union branches, trades councils, Labour Party Constituency branches[133], various working-class organisations and papers, and individual trade unionists, in one way or another contributed to the cause by putting pressure on their national executives to take action or to disseminate knowledge about the situation.

The following letter from the TUC is a small victory:

"We are pursuing our enquiries into the trade union situation in Iran, but our General Council have not to date issued a statement on that matter. From the information currently available we have noted that the workers' organisations in Iran are closely aligned with the single ruling party, and the International Confederation of Free Trade Unions takes the view that there are no independent trade unions in that country."[134] (Our emphasis)

---

132. Letter from the International Department of the TUC to CRTURI, May 5, 1976.

133. Many Labour Party Constituency Parties have already supported CRTURI in various ways. One form of this support has been sending numerous resolutions to NEC and demanding that NEC should give every possible assistance to the struggle of the workers in Iran and support CRTURI in their campaign against the Shah's brutal regime.

The Massey-Ferguson workers in the Bannery Lane plant have taken a lead in this country in recognising how their bargaining power can be weakened

cntd...

This is a beginning - and can be called a victory insomuch as the TUC has acknowledged that problems exist and that they are now starting to do something about them; but it is an extremely small victory because there is still so much to be done.

A Sample of Iranian Industrial Relations in this Country

What the Iranian government does in Iran has already been extended to Britain in the case of the dispute between ASTMS and Iran Air[135]. British employees

---

133.cntd... by the weak and unorganised bargaining power of the workers in Iran. Because of this understanding at a conference organised by their strike committee on March 1, 1977, a speaker from the Campaign was given the courtesy of time at the meeting. The following resolution which was moved by the CRTURI speaker was carried unanimously:

"That this meeting being mindful of the apalling conditions under which the workers of Iran fight for democratic trade unions, and also of the fact that the active solidarity of the British workers is vital to the success of the fight against the brutal dictatorship of the Shah, calls on the TUC and all national trade unions,

1. to find out about the conditions under which trade unionists in Iran fight for better living and working conditions;

2. to put pressure on the companies already in Iran, such as Chrysler's, Leyland's and Massey-Ferguson's, to release information about wages and conditions of work in Iran;

3. to give all possible publicity and assistance to the trade unionists and workers who are carrying on this struggle and being shot down, imprisoned and tortured because of their fight for basic human rights in Iran."

134. Letter from the General Secretary, TUC to CRTURI, March 15, 1976.

135. See what International Kayhan, (February 13, 1977) the semi-official newspaper, has to say about ASTMS:

"This union has a reputation in England for harsh and extremist tendencies."

of Iran Air have been struggling for the right to be represented by a British trade union.

The following statement issued by ASTMS to the customers of Iran Air in January, 1977, speaks for itself:

> "The service you have enjoyed from Iran Air has been provided by the dedication and professionalism of the Staff."
>
> "This service can only be continued if the Staff are allowed the same Freedom as the majority of other airline workers, to join a British Trade Union, and bargain collectively on their terms of service."
>
> "Every major political party in this country has urged <u>every</u> employee to join a Trade Union and actively participate in it's affairs."
>
> "Iran Air have persistantly refused to recognise our Union and advised many of us that our careers would not be secure if we became members of a Trade Union and participate in it's affairs."
>
> "This attitude is a direct contravention of this country's public policy."
>
> "We regret any inconvenience you have suffered and would ask you to assist us to return to work by advising Iran Air that they should recognise the Union and allow it's Staff to participate or it will lose your custom forever."

This is further proof of what we have been saying about the regime; and it is a warning to British trade unionists of the kind of treatment which they could expect if they took jobs within Iranian firms whether in Iran or in this country, because the attitude of Iran Air is a direct reflection of Iranian government policy. But we must add that because of the adverse publicity which Iran Air received over this dispute we believe that they will make a settlement along ASTMS terms.

3. Visits to Iran

Finally we deal with the Embassy's offer of visits to Iran. The first prerequisite of any investigation is that the investigators can freely inquire into all aspects of the problems they are interested in - in this case, Iranian working and living conditions and the nature and work of the government-controlled trade unions - and that the workers can freely express their real opinions and grievances. It becomes obvious, given the present situation in Iran that no Embassy-supervised and financed trip can enable British trade unionists to see the real conditions of their brothers and sisters in Iran. We also want to counteract the impressions which have been gained already by a few visitors to Iran who have been mislead by carefully shepherded visits to showplace factories and farms[136]. These people forget that they have been carefully supervised. If they asked for comments from workers they were not aware of - or they forgot - the government employees, the managers or employers, and the SAVAK agents, who were standing beside them listening to the answers to the questions; in such circumstances, where dissent leads straight to unemployment or even gaol and possible torture, what does the visitor expect the Iranian worker to say?

It is necessary to look behind the facade - after all, Mussolini was praised for getting the Italian trains to run on time, and Hitler had some very efficient factories as well as gas ovens - and to probe widely and deeply into the economic and political life of Iran and into the working-class movement.

Do such visitors really want to give respectability to one of the "most repressive regimes in the world"?

---

136. CRTURI has already made clear its position toward the Chrysler Shop Steward visit to Iran at the February Coventry Trades Council Meeting and we have collected a good deal of material on this visit but this deserves a separate analysis.

Of course, not all visitors are starry-eyed; there was the Midlands Manager from an engineering firm who reported that on a visit to Tehran he was escorted everywhere by the secret police - and he said he would not take a job in Iran for £1,000 a week!

The repressive regime in Iran is desperate for recognition by western trade unionists and is canvassing throughout the world to enlist western trade unionists and intellectuals in its cause so that they will paint the ugly, repressive nature of the regime in glowing colours, thus justifying the Shah's brutal actions.

The following statement by the Hackney Trades Council, after being offered a "sponsored" visit by the Iranian Embassy in February, 1977, is the correct answer to such offers:

> "The EC recommends that we do not accept the invitation to visit Iran unless - and this would have to be very carefully proved before anyone went - there is absolute freedom to speak to anyone, to visit what we think fit, i.e. we don't go. It would be like accepting an invitation from Hitler to visit the Third Reich! "[137]

---

137. Hackney Trades Council Report, February, 1977. Mr E. McCluskey, Chrysler Coventry Steward, should hear this!

APPENDIX I

TEXT OF IRAN'S LABOUR LAW

Together with many other Constituency Labour Party branches (and trade unions, trades councils and other labour movement organisations) Reigate CLP protested to the Iranian Embassy in London about the living and working conditions of their brothers and sisters in Iran and about the persecution of trade unionists in that country.

They received the following letter in reply:

IMPERIAL IRANIAN EMBASSY

16, PRINCES GATE,
LONDON, S.W.7.
TEL. 01-584 8101

Ref : 104 E

19th January, 1977

Mrs. M. Neville,
Reigate Constituency Labour Party,
Progress House,
164 Garlands Road,
Redhill,
SURREY RH1 6NZ.

Dear Mrs. Neville,

With reference to your letter of 14th January, 1977 to the Iranian Ambassador in respect of information concerning Trade Unionists in Iran.

Enclosed please find copy of the Labour Law of Iran together with a copy of Iran's Programme for Expansion of Industrial Ownership which I turst will be of some assistance to you in understanding the situation and conditions of the workers, farmers and the general public in Iran. I am sure after perusal of the above there will be no further protests from your Party.

If further information is needed by you as per the above I would be pleased to hear from you.

Yours sincerely,

J. Bahar

Jalil Bahar
Economic Counsellor

Enc.

WE REPRINT HERE THE EXACT TEXT OF THE LABOUR LAW AS RECEIVED BY REIGATE CLP FROM THE EMBASSY

LABOUR LAW OF IRAN

(Approved by the joint committee of the Houses of Parliament on 17th March 1959 and ammended on 9th February 1965)

CHAPTER ONE

GENERAL PROVISION

Article 1. For purposes of this Law, a worker is a person who works in any designation under the instructions of an employer against receipt of salary or wages.

Note Persons to whom the provisions of the Civil Service Act or other laws and regulations concerning employment are applicable shall not be subject to the provisions of this Act.

Article 2. For purposes of this Law the term "apprentice" shall apply to those individuals who have not attained eighteen full years of age and are under a written apprenticeship contract, engaged in a working place and or special classes for a definite period not exceeding 2 years, with the object of completing or learning a special trade or art.

Article 3. An employer is a real or juridical person under whose instruction or for whose account a worker works.

Managers and responsible persons and generally all persons entrusted with the duty of running the working place, shall be regarded as the employer's representatives, and the employer is responsible for carrying out all the obligations undertaken by such representatives toward the workers.

Article 4. Wage and salary consist of cash payment made and non-pecuniary allowances granted to worker against performance of work.

Article 5. A working place is a place where a worker works under the instructions of an employer such as public places, industrial, mining, constructional, commercial, freight & passenger transport institutions and the like.

All installations such as dining halls, bathrooms, dispensaries, gymnasiums, vocational training schools, and the like which, by the exigency of the work, belong to the working place shall also be considered as a part of the working place.

Article 6. All workers, employers and working places shall be subject to the provisions of this Act.

Note 1. The Ministry of Labour may temporarily exempt working places with less than ten workers from part of the provisions of this Act.

Note 2. Duration of work, holidays and leaves, wage or salary of fishermen, sailors, crews, airport workers, pilots, technicians and employees working in the aeroplanes or workers whose type of work is such that their wages and earnings are partly or entirely provided through customers or clients; dock workers as well as workers whose type of work requires working on shift basis shall be specified under separate regulations.

Note 3. Should the provisions of the Labour Law be not applicable to the work conditions of the workers of some trades and workshops, the Ministry of Labour and Social Affairs shall draw a special set of regulations applicable to the said workers' work conditions, after taking into account the views of the workers' and employers' organisations and obtaining the confirmation of the High Labour Council, and shall enforce such regulations after they have been passed by the labour committee of the two Houses of the Parliament.

Article 7. Family working places in which the work is exclusively performed by the owner himself and his blood relatives of first grade from first category shall not be subject to the provisions of this Act.

Article 8. Agricultural workers and house-maids and servants shall be subject to special provisions to be specified under separate acts.

Article 9. Employers are bound to prepare and submit, in accordance with the relevant regulations, all statistics and data required by the Ministry of Labour.

Article 10. Foreign subjects can not be engaged in any work in Iran, unless they are granted permission to do so under the relevant laws and regulations of the country and obtain official work permit from the Ministry of Labour in accordance with the relevant regulations.

Note 1. The following persons, by the virture of the posts or titles they hold, and while they hold such posts and titles, shall not, with the approval of the Ministry of Labour and Social Affairs, have to obtain a work permit.

1 - Employees and experts of the United Nations and its affiliated organisations.

2 - Reporters of foreign press and news agencies with the provision of a reciprocity, and also provided that they are, in the opinion of the Ministry of Information, reporters by profession.

Note 2. The staffs of foreign authorised cultural, health, and development institutions, provided that such institutions are in no way profit organisations and their staffs receive no money from Iranian Government, institutions and citizens as wages or salaries, shall obtain free work permits.

Note 3. With joint approval of the Ministries of Interior and Foreign Affairs and in accordance with the employment regulations for foreign citizens, free work permits shall be issued for refugees.

Note 4. Employers and institutions may not employ foreign citizens who do not hold work permits.

Note 5. The Government may, when necessary or as a term of reciprocity, by the proposal of the Ministry of Labour and Social Affairs and the approval of the Board of Ministers, exempt the citizens of a foreign country from paying the dues for the issuance or renewal of their work permits.

Note 6. The amount of the cash fine provided for in article 59 of the Labour Law concerning the violation of article 10 of the same law and its notes is thus raised to Rls. 20,000.

CHAPTER TWO

DURATION OF WORK

Article 11. The working hours of workers in working places, with the exception of the instances specified in this Act, shall not exceed 8 hours per day and 48 hours per week. By "working hours" is meant the period during which a worker is at the disposal of the employer for performing duty. Rest periods as well as the time spent for meals, shall not be considered as part of the working hours.

Note 1. Various types of hard and injurious works which require that a worker should work less than 8 hours per day shall be specified under special regulations.

Note 2. The employer may, on some days of the week, fix the working hours at less than 8 hours, and increase the working hours on other days of the week, provided that the working hours do not exceed 9 hours per day and 48 hours per week.

Note 3. In respect of shift work, the working hours may exceed 8 hours per day and 48 hours per week, provided that the total working hours in four consecutive weeks of work do not exceed 192 hours.

Article 12. Overtime work shall be allowed by mutual agreement of both parties and with due regard to the following conditions:

1. For every hour of overtime work, an additional payment of 35% of per hour wage shall be made to the worker.
2. Overtime work shall not exceed 4 hours per day.
3. Overtime work is forbidden in hard and injurious works.

Note. The assignment of any kind of overtime work to children under 16 years of age is forbidden.

Article 13. In the event of the occurrence of an accident and or necessary repairs in the working place and or machinery and force-majeure, the employer may, as an exception, keep all or a number of the workers for overtime work, paying them the overtime allowance provided in Article 12.

CHAPTER THREE

HOLIDAYS AND LEAVE

Article 14. In each week, Friday shall be the rest day of workers with pay. Where with the consent of the worker - another day of the week be fixed permanently as the rest day, such day shall be considered as weekly rest-day.

Note. Workers who work on Friday, shall be entitled to rest on another day of the week with pay. In the case of non-shift workers who work on Friday; if they are granted another day of the week as rest day, they shall receive additional payment of 35% but if no other rest day is granted, with the consent of the worker, they shall be paid 135% in addition to the ordinary daily wages.

Article 15. Every worker shall be entitled to 12 days leave with pay against twelve months of work. In the case of workers under 16 full years of age, the period of leave with pay, shall be 18 days against twelve months of work. Fridays and official labour holidays, shall not be included in the workers' leave period. The following days shall be considered as official holidays with pay:-

New Year's Day (No-Ruz)
13th day of Farvadin
Labour Day
Anniversary of the Constitution
Ashoora
21th (sic) of Ramazan
Id-i Qurban
Id-i Ghadir
H.I.M.'s Birthday
28th of Safar (the day of the Prophet's death and of Imam Hassan's martyrdom)

Note 1. The basis of calculation of leave and holiday pay in respect of piece-workers (receiving piece-wages) shall be one-half of the average piece wage paid to the worker during the last thirty days of work, provided that in no case, shall this amount be less than the minimum wage.

Note 2. Should utilization of a worker's annual leave be postponed to the next year, using of leave shall be binding for the worker. The date of the leave shall be fixed by mutual consent. In the absence of such a consent the decision of the relative Factory Council shall be final and binding.

Note 3. In the event of a worker's abandonment of work or his dismissal or death and or closing down of the working place, the employer shall be bound to pay wages for the period of leave which has accrued to him in proportion to the number of months of his service.

CHAPTER FOUR

CONDITIONS OF WORK OF WOMEN AND CHILDREN

Article 16. Employment of children under 12 years of age, even for apprenticeship purposes shall be forbidden.

Article 17. Night work (between hours of 22 and 6) for women and workers below 18 years of age shall be forbidden, except in the case of nurses of hospitals and such other jobs as will be specified at the discretion of the Ministry of Labour.

Article 18. Pregnant women are forbidden to work during the period between 6 weeks prior to and four weeks after child-birth and the employer shall not have the right to discharge them during the said period.

Article 19. The employer is bound to grant nursing mothers half an hour break at the end of every three hours of work for the purpose of nursing their children. Such break periods shall be regarded as part of their working hours, where the number of such children in one working place exceeds 10 persons the employer shall be bound to allocate a place for keeping them.

Article 20. Assignment of hard and injurious works to children under 18 years of age and to women shall be forbidden.

CHAPTER FIVE

WAGE AND SALARY

Article 21. Wage or salary shall be paid to the workers at the end of each week or fortnight on working days at the working place.

Note 1. Where part of a wage or salary is non-pecuniary, the manner of delivery thereof shall be subject to mutual agreement of both parties.

Note 2. Wages of workers employed on shift duty throughout the month shall be ten percent more than the wages of similar non-shift workers.

Note 3. Only non-shift workers shall be entitled to 35% in addition to their wages for ordinary hours of work, for each hour of work performed during the night (between 22 and 6 hours).

Article 22. The minimum wage of a non-qualified (ordinary) worker shall, with due regard to essential requirements and cost of living in various parts of the country, be such that will meet the living expenses of one man, one wife and two children.

The minimum wage in various parts of the country and in industries shall be proposed, in accordance with a special regulation, by a committee composed of the representatives of government, employer and workers and shall be put into effect after confirmation by the Ministry of Labour and the approval of the High Labour Council. So long as the new minimum wagé is not ascertained the former minimum wage shall remain valid.

Note. Employers shall be bound, for the purposes of wages, to classify various jobs of their working place.

Article 23. Wages of female and male workers shall be equal for equal work.

Article 24. The workers' wages shall rank as the employer's priority dues, needing to be provided for and paid in preference to other debts, even his tax dues. No more than $\frac{1}{4}$ of the workers wages can be attached in satisfaction of debt, nor may the worker himself apply for a deduction of more than $\frac{1}{4}$ of his wages in satisfaction of any sum due by him, unless he has incurred such a debt through purchase of living necessities from cooperative societies.

The expenses of maintenance of the worker's wife, children and others who are entitled to receive his support are an exception to the above rule and shall be subject to the provisions of the Civil Code.

CHAPTER SIX

SYNDICATES

Article 25. A syndicate is an organisation established by the workers of a profession or a workshop, by the employers of a trade or an industry and also by members of a free profession, in order to protect their professional interests and improve their economic and social status. Combination of several syndicates will form a union and that of several unions will form a confederation.

Article 26. All syndicates, unions and confederations are bound, at the time of formation, to draw up a constitution and submit it to the Ministry of Labour for registration. The Ministry of Labour shall agree to the registration of such associations provided their constitutions are not in conflict with the provisions of this Act and its relevant Regulation.

Note. Syndicates, unions and confederations which have, prior to the ratification of this Act, been registered with the Ministry of Labour, are bound, within a period of three months from the date of enforcement of this Act, to have their constitutions conform to the provisions of this Chapter and the relevant Regulation, and duly notify the Ministry of Labour for re-registration.

Article 27. Main rights and functions of syndicates, unions and confederations shall be as follows:

a) To conclude collective labour contracts.

b) To purchase, sell and require movable and immovable properties, provided it is not for commercial purposes and with a view to gain profit.

c) To defend the trade rights and interests of their members.

d) To establish co-operative societies to meet the requirements of their members.

e) To establish and create unemployment funds for the purpose of giving aid and assistance to unemployed workers. Other rights and functions as well as other provisions concerning the constitution, the manner of formation, registration and dissolution of the syndicates unions and confederations shall be specified under the relevant regulation.

Article 28. It shall be forbidden to coerce, force and menace workers to accept membership of a syndicate and or prevent them from acceptance of such a membership.

Article 29. Syndicates, unions and confederations shall not be entitled to interfere in political affairs. They may however in cases of safeguarding their trade and economic interests express tendancies towards and cooperate with political parties.

CHAPTER SEVEN

LABOUR CONTRACT

Article 30. By "labour contract" is meant a written or verbal agreement under which a worker undertakes, against wage, to perform a work for an employer for a definite or indefinite period.

Article 31. Benefits provided under labour contract shall in no way be less than those provided for workers in this Act.

Article 32. Where the labour contract is concluded for a definite period or for the performance of a definite work neither party may unilaterally cancel the contract, except in the cases expressly provided therein.

Any of the two parties cancelling the contract in other than the above cases shall be bound to indemnify the other party.

Article 33. Where the labour contract is concluded for an indefinite period, either party can cancel the contract on giving 15 days prior notice in writing. Where the discharged worker has worked for an employer for a period of one year, either successively or alternately, on cancellation of the contract the employer shall pay him, for each year of his service, an amount equivalent to 15 days of the last wages.

A dismissed worker having served for an employer for a minimum period of three consecutive months or six alternative months before the termination of his service, has the right to complain within fifteen days, to the authorities specified under the Chapter on Settlement of Disputes of this Act. The authorities mentioned therein may, in addition to the payment specified above and with due regard to the length of service, rate of pay, age, number of worker's dependents, and other conditions and circumstances, award by way of compensation an amount not exceeding the total of three years wages of the worker. The employer shall have the option to pay the said compensation or to reinstate the worker and pay his wage for the days of his suspension.

Note 1. The provisions of this Article shall not effect the labour contracts which have been concluded for a definite period or for the performance of a definite work.

Note 2. The dismissal of a workers' representative duly elected under the provisions of Article 44 of the Labour Law, and the dismissal of the Secretary or Members of the Board of Directors of the workers' Syndicate or a change in their job, such that they may be unable to perform their legal functions, shall be subject to the prior and written approval of the Ministry of Labour and Social Affairs. Dismissal of qualified candidates for workers' representative within the period specified for election shall be subject to the above-mentioned provisions.

Article 34. Where on the finding of the Board of Settlement of Disputes, the dismissal of a worker is due to his fault or negligence in the performance of his duties, he shall not be entitled to any right.

CHAPTER EIGHT

COLLECTIVE BARGAINING CONTRACTS

Article 35. By "collective bargaining contract" is meant a written agreement concluded between one or several labour syndicates, unions, or confederations on the one part and one or several employers or employers' syndicates, unions or confederations on the other part, for the purpose of determining conditions of work.

Benefits provided under a collective bargaining contract shall in no way be less than those provided for in this Act.

Article 36. The authority for investigating the disputes arising out of collective bargaining contracts shall in the first instance be the Disputes Settlement Board and in the final instance, the High Labour Council.

CHAPTER NINE

SETTLEMENT OF DISPUTES

Article 37. In the event of a dispute between an employer and a worker or an apprentice arising from the enforcement of the provisions of this Act or from a labour contract or an apprenticeship contract, such disputes shall, in the first instance, be settled directly by reconciliation between the employer and the worker or the apprentice and or their respective representatives.

Article 38. Where the dispute is not settled by reconciliation, the complainant shall refer the matter to the local Department of Labour, and the said Department shall, within three days of receiving the complaint, refer the matter to the resprective Factory Council.

The Factory Council shall consist of representative of the Ministry of Labour, one representative of the employer and one representative of the workers of the same working place. This Council is bound to investigate the dispute and announce its decision within one week. The decisions of the Factory Council shall be considered as final and binding, except where it concerns wages and or dismissal of a worker and or compensation of material losses incurred by the employer due to the action of the worker, in which case the matter may be referred to the Disputes Settlement Board within a period of ten days from the date of communication of the said decision.

Note. In working places where a Factory Council has not been set up, the Department of Labour is bound to investigate the dispute in the presence of the complainant and the disputing party or their representative. The award issued by the Department of Labour shall have the same validity as that issued by the Factory Council.

Article 39. In the event of the representative of workers or the employers not attending the meeting of the Factory Council, another meeting shall be held within a maximum period of five days. At this meeting the Representative of the Ministry of Labour and the representative attending the meeting shall give their votes. If a unanimous vote is not obtained, the matter shall be referred to the Disputes Settlement Board.

Article 40. The Disputes Settlement Board shall consist of three representatives of the Government (Governor, the local Chief Justice, Head of the Department of Labour or their representatives). Three workers' representatives and three employers' representative.(sic) Each one of the aforementioned groups shall have one vote and the vote given by the majority shall rule. The Governor shall preside over the Disputes Settlement Board and in his absence the Head of the Department of Labour shall take his place.

Note 1. In the event of a diversity of opinions among members of one of the groups, individual voting shall be carried out. The decisions adopted by majority of votes of the individuals present, shall be decisive. In the event of a tie, the vote of the group which includes the representative of the Ministry of Labour shall be final and binding.

Note 2. The Ministry of Labour may, where necessary, set up several Disputes Settlement Boards in the same olcality as in the manner specified above.

Article 41. Where the negligence or fault of a worker causes an accident and or destruction of an (sic) damage to one of the tools and equipments of the working place, or diminishes the product, the employer shall have the right to demand from the worker through the Factory Council and the Disputes Settlement Board compensation for the loss incurred.

Article 42. In the event that the representatives of the Government, or employers or workers do not attend the meeting of the Disputes Settlement Board, another meeting shall be held within a period of three days. Implausible absence of the Government representatives from meetings of the Disputes Dettlement Board shall be considered as an administrative offense. Absence of employers', or workers' representatives from two consecutive meetings shall be considered as their resignation.

Article 43. Final awards issued by the Facto.y Council and the Disputes Settlement Board shall be binding and shall be enforced through the Executive Office of the Courts of Justice. The procedure relating thereto shall be laid down under a Regulation which shall upon the proposal of the Ministries of Labour and Justice, be approved by the Council of Ministers.

Article 44. The procedure concerning election of representatives of workers and employers and their alternates as well as other provisions relating to this Chapter, shall be laid down under separate regulations.

Article 44 Bis. Should the workers' or employers' organisations stated in Article 25 gain majority in a workshop or a trade, in the opinion of the Ministry of Labour and Social Affairs, the said Ministry can, in instances deemed necessary, entrust the legal duties and authorities of the representatives of workers and employers to the said workers' and employers' organisations.

Article 45. In the event of collective dispute arising between workers and employer, the local Department of Labour shall take immediate measures for holding a meeting to be attended by representatives of the workers and the employer in order to bring about a reconciliation between the two parties. If the dispute is not settled in the above manner, the local Department of Labour shall immediately refer the matter to the Disputes Settlement Board. The said Board shall investigate the matter and make recommendations to both parties within a period of ten days for the settlement of the dispute.
Note. By "collective dispute" mentioned in this Article is meant a dispute which would disturb or sever the employer-worker relations in a workshop and which would possibly result in a "lock-out" (by the employer) or a "strike" (by the workers).

Article 46. Where the two parties refuse to accept the recommendations of the Disputes Settlement Board within a period of three days, the Head of the Department of Labour is bound to report the matter immediately to the Ministry of Labour for adoption of the necessary decision. Where necessary the Council of Ministers may so long as the dispute has not been settled, operate the working place on behalf of the employer in any manner as it may deem appropriate.

Article 46 Bis. The authorities to settle the collective disputes between workers and employers of public services such as water, electricity and public transportation, and the manner in which such disputes are to be settled, shall be determined by a set of special regulations drawn with a view to the needs and well-being of the public and approved by the High Labour Council.

CHAPTER TEN

INDUSTRIAL SAFETY & OCCUPATIONAL HEALTH

Article 47. To draw up and approve regulations providing for occupational health and workers safety and the prevention of accidents in working areas a board named "High Safety Council" composed of the following persons shall be set up in the Ministry of Labour:-

1. The Minister of Labour or his Under-Secretary who shall preside over the Council at the meeting.
2. The Under-Secretary of the Ministry of Interior.
3. The Under-Secretary of Justice.
4. The Under-Secretary of the Ministry of Industries & Mines.
5. The Under-Secretary of the Ministry of Public Health.
6. The Master of Engineering College of Teheran University.
7. The Head or Official in charge of the Department of Labour Standards and Inspection who shall also act as the Secretary of the Council.

The said Council may, when necessary, take measures to set up committees of conversant and well informed experts for drawing up the relevant regulations.

Note 1. Internal regulations for the High Safety Council shall be proposed by the Secretary of the Council and shall be enforced after approval by the Council.

Note 2. Attendance fees for the members of the High Safety Council and the relevant committees shall be determined by the Ministry of Labour.

Article 48. Those wishing to establish new working places and or extend existing working places are bound first to submit their work programme, construction plans and contemplated projects for the approval of the Ministry of Labour to ensure safety and occupational health. The operation of such working places shall be subject to the observance of the safety and health provisions.

Article 49. Employers are bound to obtain required permission from the Ministry of Labour before using those parts of the tools and equipment which are required to be tested under the Regulations passed by the High Safety Council. Where such tools and equipment are used without permission, the offending employer shall be sentenced to the punishment prescribed in the later part of Article 60. Where such tools and equipment are found to be dangerous or harmful on grounds of health and industrial safety a public Investigator shall, at the request of the Ministry of Labour, issue detention orders in respect thereof.

Article 50. Where in the course of inspection by the Labour Inspector he perceives the risk of occurence of an accident or the arising of a danger in a working place the Public Investigator shall, at the request of the Ministry of Labour and in accordance with the provisions of Law, issue award for the shutdown of all or part of the working places. In each case orders for reopening of the working places shall be issued by the public Investigator or by the Court immediately upon production of the Ministry of Labour's certificate concerning the fitness of the working place to resume operations.
Note. The employer is bound to pay the wages of his workers who are directly or indirectly rendered idle during each shutdown.

Article 51. Persons sustaining loss as a result of the above awards can appeal to the local Court of First Instance within 24 hours of the date on which the public Investigator's award is served. The Court is bound to investigate the case immediately and its decision in such cases shall be provisionally enforceable.

CHAPTER ELEVEN

LABOUR INSPECTION

Article 52. For the enforcement of the provisions of this Act the Ministry of Labour shall appoint qualified persons as Labour Inspectors. The Labour Inspectors shall have the right to enter the working-places covered by this Act at any time and carry out their inspection. The report of the Labour Inspectors shall, in so far as it concerns the enforcement of this Act, have the same validity as those of judicial functionaries.

Employers and workers are bound to comply with all safety and health regulations.

Rules concerning the method of inspection, industrial safety and health as well as duties and powers of the Labour Inspectors shall be specified under special regulations.

Article 53. Labour Inspectors shall in no case, even after detachment from the government service, have the right to divulge the commercial and technical secrets which they obtain by virtue of their office or to disclose the names of persons who have informed them of cases of infringement. Those violating the provisions of this Article, shall be liable to the punishment prescribed under Article 220 of the Penal Code.

CHAPTER TWELVE

HIGH LABOUR COUNCIL

Article 54. A Council known as "High Labour Council" shall be formed in the Ministry of Labour whose functions shall consist of approval of executive regulations for the enforcement of this Act as well as carrying out any other functions which under the provisions of this Act and other relevant laws and regulations, have been assigned to the High Labour Council.

Article 55. The High Labour Council shall be appointed for a period of two years and will be composed of following persons:

a) Three representatives of the Government who shall be the Minister of Labour or his Under-Secretary and two persons well conversant with social and economic problems, to be nominated by the Minister of Labour and approved by the Council of Ministers.

b) Employer syndicates registered in accordance with this Act employers having a minimum number of 500 workers, shall each nominate one representative to the Ministry of Labour. The Minister of Labour shall appoint from among the nominated representatives three persons as principal members and three persons as alternate members to set on the High Labour Council.(sic)

c) Workers' syndicates registered in accordance with this Act shall each nominate a representative to the Ministry of Labour. The Minister of Labour shall appoint from among such nominees or from among workers' representatives on Factory Councils, three persons to act as principal members and three persons as alternate members.

Article 56. Meetings of the High Labour Council shall be held at the invitation of and presided over by the Minister of Labour or his Under-Secretary.

Dicisions(sic) of the Council shall be adopted by majority of votes, and each of the three groups, i.e. workers' employers' and Government representatives, shall have one vote. If no majority vote is obtained among the members of one group, individual voting shall be taken and the majority vote shall prevail.

The internal regulation of the High Labour Council shall be proposed by the Minister of Labour and shall be enforceable after approval by the High Labour Council.

Note. The Ministry of Labour shall be bound to make arrangements for the appointment of the members of the next council three months before the expiry of the term of office of the previous one.

CHAPTER THIRTEEN

OFFENSES AND PENALTIES

Article 57. Where the employer does not submit to the Ministry of Labour the satistics and data provided for in Article 9 of this Act, he shall in each instance, be liable to payment of a fine of Rls. 500 to Rls. 5000.

Article 58. Any employer violating the provisions of Articles 11, 12, 14, 15, 21, 22 and 23 of this Act and the relevant regulations, shall, in each case be liable to payment of a fine of Rls. 1000 to Rls. 10,000. The maximum of the above fine shall apply to cases of assigning overtime work to workers under the age of 16.

Article 59. Those offending against the provisions of Article 10 and its relevant regulation as well as employers violating the provisions of Chapter IV of this Act and its relevant regulations, shall, in each case, be liable to payment of a fine of Rls. 1000 to Rls. 10,000 or to correctional imprisonment ranging from one month to two months or to both punishments.

Employers guilty of employing children below twelve years of age shall be sentenced to the maximum of both of the above punishments.

Article 60. Employers or persons who prevent the Labour Inspectors to perform duty, from entering working places which are subject to this Act, or those who refrain from furnishing them with the required information and documents, shall, in each case, be liable to payment of a fine of Rls. 1000 to Rls. 10,000. In the event of the failure of the employer to comply with the rules and regulations concerning health and safety he shall in each case be liable to payment of a fine of Rls. 5.000 to Rls. 100,000.

Article 61. Any person who by force and threat or by using, coercion comples (sic) another to accept membership of a syndicate and or keeps him from joining a syndicate, shall be liable to payment of a fine of Rls. 1,000 to Rls. 10,000 or a term of correctional imprisonment ranging from one month to two months or to both punishments.

Article 62. Any person who in contravention of the provisions of the International Labour Conventions Nos. 29 and 105 sets another person to forced labour shall, in addition to payment of due wages be in each case sentenced to payment of a fine of Rials. 1,000 to Rls. 10,000 or to a term of correctional imprisonment ranging from one month to six months or to both punishments.

Article 63. The fines prescribed in this Chapter, shall be paid into a special account in a bank, and such funds shall be spent for the welfare of workers, under the supervision of the Minister of Labour and in accordance with a regulation to be approved by the Council of Minsiters.

Article 64. The representative of the Ministry of Labour shall have the right to attend the court when such cases are being heard and to plead the case for the Ministry of Labour.

CHAPTER FOURTEEN

MISCELLANEOUS PROVISIONS

Article 65. The Ministry of Labour may supervise the method of operation of the private employment agencies and gradually establish free state employment agencies.

Article 66. Employers shall arrange for making all necessary facilities available in the working place in order to train experienced individuals and to raise the standard of technical knowledge and skill of their workers and apprentices in accordance with the relevant regulations.

Article 67. The Ministry of Labour shall draw up all the regulations for the enforcement of this Act and shall put them into effect after approval by the High Labour Council. However, the regulations affecting Article 10, 43 and 63 shall be enforceable after the approval by the Council of Ministers, and regulations to Chapter Ten (Industrial Safety and Occupational Health) shall be enforceable after the approval by the High Safety Council.

Article 68. From the date of approval of this Act, the Law approved on 17th Khordad 1328 authorizing implementation of the report by the Majlis Committee of Commerce and Industries dated 11th Esfand 1327 and any other enactments inconsistent with this Act shall be repealed.

Article 69. The Ministries of Labour and Justice are charged with the duty of enforcing the provisions of this Act.

APPENDIX II
MULTINATIONALS

> "U.K. business can only become interested in the opportunities for investment in Iran where profits can be made and workers are not allowed to strike."[138]

We are able to give a few of the companies which have concluded new agreements with Iran for production within Iran:

Acrow (Engineering) have concluded an agreement with Iran for the production of a range of fabricated equipment for petro-chemical and oil industries as produced by the Adamson Division of Acrow.

British Industrial Plastics produces formaldehyde, amino moulding powder and urea formaldehyde resins.

British Leyland has also concluded an agreement for the production of double-decker buses with the Leyland Motors of Iran.

> "Leyland Motors Iran have plans to export several double-decker buses to an African market."

Some believe that this unspecified market is South Africa.

Morratab Company have expanded their Landrover production.

Morgan Grenfell and Company Limited have established branches in Iran.

International Agricultural Development Corporation (UK) Limited.

Hawker Siddeley produces a full range of Hawker Siddeley in Iran. It was intended the products reach 12,500 units annually.

International Compressed Air Corporation (Compair) which produces compressed air equipment in Iran, half for domestic and half for export markets.

Joseph Lucas Industries, produces automative electrical equipment in Ghazwim.

London Rubber Industries, production of household, industrial and surgical rubber gloves.

---

138. Financial Times, July 28, 1975.

Massey-Ferguson, tractors and other Massey-Ferguson equipment are produced in Tahriz. Massey-Ferguson produces both for home and foreign market.

Tractor Manufacturing Company of Iran made a 4 million contract with Forging Developments of Bromsgrove.

LEP with London Brick Company Limited are building a brick factory which will produce about 1 million bricks a day.

Glynwed will establish a joint company with Iranian capitalists.

Giltspur Engineering Consultants Limited are building a freezer in Shiraz.

Crane Aid Services (CAS) is to sign a 3 million contract for the restoration and repair of Khoramshahr Port.

BAC:

> "After eight months of highly complex negotiations, BAC tonight signed an agreement here for the first ever large scale arms supply deal to be paid for in oil by the Iranian Government. The deal involves the supply by BAC of the tracked Rapier missile - a deal worth £400m. - over £100m. more than when first revealed last December."[139]

British Oxygen, Flower Group, International Agricultural Development Corporation (UK) Limited, Bovis Limited, International Combustion Division, Derby, GEC Turbine Generators Limited, GEC-Elliot Process Automation, Richard Costain Limited.

---

139. The Financial Times, Friday, November 19, 1976.

List of participants at the Iran United Kingdom Industrial Conference 1973
Takhte-Jamshid, Iran November 25-30, 1973.

Executive Committee: United Kingdom

The Rt Hon Peter Walker,
Secretary of State for Trade & Industry
Sir Michael Clapham,
President, Confederation of British Industry - Deputy-Chairman, Imperial Chemical Industries Ltd
Lord Stokes,
Chairman, British Leyland Motor Corp Ltd
Sir Monty Prichard, (represented by Mr F. Wilkinson),
Chairman & Managing Director, Perkins Engines Group Ltd

The Rt Hon The Lord Thorneycroft,
Chairman, British Overseas Trade Board - Chairman, Pirelli Ltd - Chairman, Pye Holdings Ltd - Chairman, Trust Houses Forte Ltd - Co-Chairman of the Conference
Mr C.D. Hamilton,
Chairman and Editor-in-Chief, Times Newspapers Ltd
Mr J.W. Buckley,
Chairman & Managing Director, Davy International Ltd

Participants and Observers

Mr B.G. Alexander,
Director, Bowater Corp Ltd
Dr D.S. Ashburner,
Davy International Ltd
Mr D. Berriman,
Managing Director, Guiness Mahon & Co Ltd
Mr J. Brennan,
Chairman, Scientific Control Systems International
Mr J. Buckingham-Burr,
Group Director, Rank-Xerox Ltd

Mr D. Alliance,
Chairman, British Northrop Ltd
Mr G.M. Bell,
Regional Controller, BLM Corp Ltd
Mr L.J. Boon,
Director, Massey-Ferguson Holdings Ltd
Mr J.P. Brown,
Planning Director, Doverstrand Ltd
Mr J.W. Buckley,
Chairman & Managing Director, Davy International Ltd

Participants and Observers continued...

Mr D.P.G. Butler,
Managing Director, Delta Metal Overseas Ltd

Lord Catto,
Chairman, Morgan Grenfell Co Ltd

Sir Michael Clapham,
President, Confederation of British Industry - Deputy Chairman, Imperial Chemical Industries Ltd

Mr J.W. Charnley,
Managing Director, John Laing Construction Ltd

Mr J.M.F. Crean,
Chairman, Unilever Export Ltd

Mr D.W. Davies,
Marketing Director, Procon Incorporated

Mr H. Davies,
Manager, Guinness Mahon & Co Ltd

Mr J. Dellal,
Managing Director, Keyser Ullman Ltd

Mr W.A. de Vigier,
Chairman, Acrow (Engineers) Ltd

Mr D. Douglas-Home,
Director, Morgan Grenfell Ltd

Mr M.J. Edwards,
Managing Director, British Steel Corp, (International) Ltd

Sir Geoffrey Eley,
Deputy Chairman, British Bank of The Middle East - Vice-Chairman, British Oxygen Co

Sir St John Elstub,
Chairman, Imperial Metal Industries Ltd

Mr G.A. Flint,
Managing Director, Adamson & Hatchett Ltd

Mr A.L. Flower,
Chairman, Flower Group of Cos

Mr P.R. Fyson,
Director & Secretary, International Compressed Air Corp Ltd

Mr T.M. Gallie,
General Manager, Marketing Dep, Imperial Metal Industries Ltd

Mr C.M. Gibson;
Managing Director, Flower Group of Cos

Mr L.C. Grand,
Planning Advisor, Barclays Bank International

Mr G.J.B. Green,
General Manager & Director, Barclays Overseas Development Corp (UK) Ltd - Director, International Agricultural Dev Corp (UK) Ltd

Participants and Observers continued...

Mr C. Gronow,
Corporate Regional Controller,
General Electric Co Ltd

Mr A. Hall-Patch,
Regional Controller, Delta Metals
Overseas Ltd

Mr C.D. Hamilton,
Chairman & Editor-in-Chief,
Times Newspapers Ltd

Mr B.E. Heggie,
Director, British Industrial Plastics
Ltd

Mr J. Holman,
Chairman, International Compressed
Air Corp Ltd

Mr R. Hutchison,
Deputy Managing Director, Bryan
Donkin Co Ltd

Mr A.G. Jackson
Group Marketing Director, Denco
Holdings Group - Vice-President,
Denco Atlas Lebanon - Director,
Denco SE

Mr M.N. John
Partner, Kennedy & Donkin

Mr D.H. Lander,
Managing Director, Chrysler
United Kingdom Ltd

Mr Frank Lee,
Managing Director, Rubery Owen
Mechanical Equipment Ltd

Mr J.F. Leishman,
Director, Hill Samuel & Co Ltd

Mr M. Littman, QC.,
Chairman, British Steel Corp
(International) Ltd

Mr J. Loudon,
Director, N M Rothschild & Sons
Ltd

Mr C.D. MacQuaide,
Group Director, Hawker-Siddeley
Group Ltd - Chairman, R A Lister
& Co Ltd

Mr R.D.C. McAlpine,
Managing Director, Baring Bros
& Co Ltd

Mr R. Mercer,
Technical Director, Delta Metal
Overseas Ltd

Mr K.W. Morley,
Market Development Advisor,
Overseas Services, British Oxygen
Co

Lord Nelson of Stafford,
Chairman, General Electric &
English Electric Cos Ltd

Mr K. Newlands,
Director, Development Policy &
Planning, British Steel Corp
(International) Ltd

Participants and Observers continued...

Mr R.D. Nutt,
Associate Partner, Brian Colquhoun & Partners

Mr W.R. Pickering,
Chairman & Managing Director, Bryan Donkin Co Ltd

Mr H.A.R. Powell,
Chairman, Massey-Ferguson Holdings Ltd

Mr T.C. Rochford,
Marketing Manager, Guest Keen & Nettlefold Ltd

Mr R.G. Roe,
Managing Director, International Agricultural Dev Corp (UK) Ltd - Managing Director, Millbank Technical Services Ltd

Mr A. Rosen,
Managing Director, Fountain Farming Ltd

Mr J.C.A. Roseveare,
Partner, Freeman, Fox & Partners

Mr D.D. Rushton,
Development Director, Fountain Farming Ltd

Rt Hon Lord Shawcross,
President, Iran Society - Chairman, Thames Television Ltd

Lord Stokes,
Chairman, British Leyland Motor Corp Ltd

Mr D.W. Stutchbury,
Managing Director, Revertex Holdings Ltd

Mr J.M. Thomas,
Chairman, Rank-Xerox Ltd

Rt Hon The Lord Thorneycroft,
Chairman, British Overseas Trade Board - Chairman, Pirelli Ltd - Chairman, Pye Holdings Ltd - Chairman, Trust Houses Forte Ltd - Co-Chairman of the Conference

Mr J.N. Thurgood,
Aladdin Iran

Mr A.W. Veness,
Sales Director, Conveyancer Ltd

Mr S.W. Wilce,
Commercial Director, Adamson & Hatchett Ltd

Mr F. Wilkinson,
Perkins Engine Group Ltd

Mr G.R.P. Willan,
Industrial Sales Director, Mirrlees Blackstone Ltd

Mr A. Wheeler,
Chairman, Conveyancer Ltd

Mr G.S.G. Witherington,
Managing Director, Reed Group Ltd

Conference Staff

Mrs Christine Azoyan,
Secretary, Ministry of Economy

Mr M. Berthoud,
British Embassy

Mrs D. Boggan,
British Embassy

Miss A. Butterworth,
CBI

Miss S. Casey,
British Embassy

Miss B. Gilpin,
CBI

Mr James Goodwin,
United Nations Expert, Ministry of Economy

Mr C.J. Gunnell,
DTI

Mr D. Mackinson,
British Embassy

Mr J. Owen,
British Embassy

Mrs P. C. Quinnen,
CBI

Mr M.V.O. Simpson-Orlebar,
British Embassy,

Mr A.F. Smith,
British Embassy

Mr J.R.E. Warburton,
CBI - Secretary General of the British Side for the organisation of the Iran-United Kingdom Investment Conference

Mrs S.A. Warburton,
CBI

Mr W. Watson,
CBI

Mr E. Worsnop,
British Embassy

APPENDIX III

WE REPRODUCE HERE A CONTEMPORARY DOCUMENT ON THE DEVELOPMENT OF THE EARLY TRADE UNIONS IN IRAN.

"SEYED MOHAMMAD DEHGAN, the head of the delegation of the trade unionists of Iran, gave the following Report[140] to the Executive Committee of the Red International of Labour Unions in January 1922:

"The first trade union was organised in Tehran in 1907. This trade union was organised by the workers in the printing trade. These workers, after a fourteen-day strike in 1918, succeeded in making a collective agreement with the employers which improved the economic conditions of the workers, and was ratified by the government. The most important achievement of this strike was the introduction of an eight-hour working day and paid overtime. This victory of the workers in the printing trade, which was organised by the Union, spurred other workers to start organising their own unions.

"Soon afterwards - namely in 1919 - Unions of Textile Workers, Shop Employees, Bakers and others were formed.

"At the present there are ten trade unions in Tehran and every day their membership is increasing. These unions are united in a Trade Unions' Council to which three elected representatives of each union belong.

"The movement has already spread in to provinces and outside Tehran trade unions[141] have been formed in Enzeli, Rasht, Ghom and Tabriz. About 8,000 workers belong to the trade unions in Tehran (which has 280,000 inhabitants of whom 50,000 are workers):

---

140. "Die Rote Gewerkschafts-Internationale", vom. 20, 1.1922: pp 171-2 Die Kommunistische Bewegung Irans. Verlag 20 May, 1973. Also Historical Documents, The Labour, Social-Democratic and Communist Movement in Iran, Volume (6), p.105, 1976, Mazdak edition.

141. Historical Documents uses "syndicate" instead of "trade union".

"

	German Edition	French Edition
1) Bakers' Union	3000	3000
2) Tailors' Union	2000	2000
3) The Cobblers' Union	1800	1800
4) The Union of Postal and Telegraph Employees	350-390	270
5) The Confectioners' Union	350-390	300
6) The Print Union	350-390	180
7) Shop Employees' Union	350-390	350
8) Office Employees' Union	350-390	250
9) Gold Embroidery Employees' Union	-	150

"In Tabriz - 200,000 inhabitants, 30,000 workers - the trade unions have 3000 members. It is to be noted that the Tabriz trade unions do not have the characteristics of genuine trade unions but tend more towards being a Workers' Party.[142]

"In Rasht - 40,000 inhabitants, 15,000 workers - the unions of printing workers and employees of cap makers (coin makers) and cobblers have about 3,500 (3000) members. In Enzeli and the suburban area the Union of Fishery Workers has about 9,000 (3,000) members of which 30 per cent are Russians. The Union of Dockers has 200 members, altogether in Enzeli and the surrounding area there are about 10,000 organised workers. As the above statistics indicate, in a short period about 20,000 workers have been organised in the trade unions in Iran. The economic situation of the workers is extremely severe. (These conditions explain the rapid development of trade unions). In addition to these conditions, in Tehran, Tabriz and several other cities, martial law was introduced[143]. In spite of all these repressions the trade unions tried to improve the workers' situation through strikes. (In the last six months there were four strikes; the bakers'

---

142. The May 20 Edition uses Workers' Party whereas Mazdak Edition uses Political Party. Further historical research has to establish which of these two terms is the true and non-falsified version of the original text of Brother Dehgan.

strike, the printers', the shop and post office employees' strike. If it is noted that the trade unions of Iran have no strike funds, and Tehran, Tabriz and Rasht are constantly under martial law, it has to be admitted that just to call for a strike is a great victory for the trade unions of Iran).

"(There are about 50,000 workers in Tehran, 30,000 in Tabriz, 15,000 in Rasht and 10,000 in Enzeli).

"The Head of the Trade Union Council of Iran, the Central Committee member SAYED MOHAMMAD DEHGAN."

---

143. But who introduced this martial law? Reza Khan. It was Reza Khan who, since the beginning of his rise to absolute despotic dictator from the time of the British coup of February, 1971, tried to suppress every manifestation of the labour movement in Iran.

Even Professor George Lenczowski in his book, Russia and the West in Iran, 1918-1948, in a sketchy fashion mentions that the movement published several newspapers of their own such as "Haqiqat" (Truth), a paper with a circulation of about 10,000. According to the Professor, Reza Shah's government closed it down and the union replaced it with "Eqtessad-I-Iran" (Economics of Iran). There is substantial evidence that at this stage the British Government, the Anglo-Persian Oil Company and Reza Shah all joined together to attempt to suppress the newly-organised trade union movement. (pp.103-4).

After half a century of trade unionism in Iran, in August 1957, Mr F.C. Mason, H.M. Counsellor (Economic) at the British Embassy, Tehran, in a book published for the Board of Trade, wrote:

"A number of syndicates and unions are officially recognised as such by the Ministry of Labour but because of the inexperience of their leaders they are not effective instruments for defending their members' interests. Although a federation of syndicates and unions, the Trades Union Congress of Iran, exists and is affiliated to the Industrial Confederation of Free Trade Unions it

cntd...

143. cntd... enjoys neither official recognition nor the support of organised labour. In general, trade union organisation is as yet too embryonic to have any material effect on working conditions."

(p.86.) (Our emphasis).

The latest example of these ex-foreign office officials who have become "expert" on Iran and who write books about Iran, is Sir Dennis Wright, and his book, recently published (1977) The English Amongst the Persians. He is an example of the "sophisticated" apologists of the Pahlavi dynasty.

SPONSORS OF THE CAMPAIGN FOR THE RESTORATION OF TRADE UNION RIGHTS IN IRAN INCLUDE:

Lawrence Daly (General Secretary, NUM), Jack Jones (General Secretary T & GWU), Alan Sapper (General Secretary ACTT), Michael McGahey (President NUM, Scottish Area), Alex Kitson (Executive Officer T & GWU), Jack Dunn (General Secretary NUM, Kent Area), Bob Wright (Assistant General Secretary AUEW-AEU), Ernie Roberts (formerly Assistant General Secretary AUEW-AEU); Lord Brockway; Labour MPs Norman Buchan, Dennis Canavan, R.F. Cook, Bryan Davies, Geoff Edge, Martin Flannery, Ted Fletcher, Judith Hart, Neil Kinnock, Russell Kerr, Arthur Latham, Tom Litterick, Eddie Loyden, Joan Maynard, Oonagh McDonald, Stan Newens, Jeff Rooker, Dennis Skinner, Ron Thomas, Audrey Wise, William Wilson; Ken Coates (Director, The Bertrand Russell Peace Foundation).

Already many trade unions, trades councils, Labour Party and LP Young Socialist branches have supported us in various ways, by resolutions, protests to the Iranian Embassy, donations, etc.

THE NATIONAL SECRETARY :

T. JALIL

The address for all communications:

BCM 816, London, W.C.1V 6XX
England.